THE ARTIST'S PALATE

The ARTIST'S

PALATE

BY NADINE HAIM

Translated from the French by Robert Erich Wolf

HARRY N. ABRAMS, INC.

Publishers, New York

To Claude
who was my great "chef"

My deep thanks go to all the artists who agreed, out of friendship, to take part in this book. It is not my book but theirs. Through the talent, knowledge, and imagination of each, whether painter or sculptor, my culinary experience has not only been enriched, but has been transformed into the stuff of art, into images.

Hearty thanks are due also to Sophie Lannes and Jean Paget for their friendly collaboration, in this case literary.

NADINE HAIM

TITLE PAGE:
Luis Marsans. *Desserts*. 1985. Mixed media on panel, 8 × 7⅛".
Private collection

LIBRARY OF CONGRESS CATALOGING-IN-PUBLICATION DATA

Haim, Nadine.
[Peintres aux fourneaux. English]
The artist's palate / by Nadine Haim : translated by Robert Erich Wolf.
p. cm.
Translation of: Peintres aux fourneaux.
Includes index.
ISBN 0-8109-1873-0
1. Cookery, International. 2. Painters. I. Title.
TX725.A1H2413 1988
641.5—dc19

87-27789
CIP

Published in 1988 by Harry N. Abrams, Incorporated, New York

A TIMES MIRROR COMPANY

Printed and bound in Japan

CONTENTS

CLAUDIO BRAVO
MCMLXXXIX

FOREWORD

Cooking is an art. Since Plato's Symposium *with its banquet of food and great talk, food has been the excuse and the occasion for philosophizing, for frivolous encounters at a table for two, for meetings held at the business lunch, or for a more restful meal outdoors where grass provides the only tablecloth.*

For Nadine Haim, it is also an act of friendly collusion, of secrets shared and consumed.

Forty-two painters and sculptors who Mrs. Haim has come to know through her brother's gallery in Paris, Galerie Claude Bernard, have contributed to this book of recipes. In doing so, they have also given us another key to appreciating their work, for in addition to their recipes, each artist has contributed a rendering of that dish in a drawing, watercolor, gouache, or oil painting.

For some of these artists the recipe recalls a favorite childhood dish, for others it suggests a journey back to the often distant lands from which they hail, and for some an attempt to cast off the loneliness of exile. For those, then, cookery has become the calendar of memory, a dream of other seasons, an excursion to other places and other years. The act of cooking is viewed as nothing less than an invitation to a voyage, a journey of the imagination, the indulgence in grave moods or flights of fancy, the sharing with others everyday.

A humble or magnificent celebration of the good things in life, food and its preparation are sometimes ascetic, sometimes distilled to their quintessence as practiced among the Chinese, or, as with the Hindus, the form a wise man's meditations may take. At times voluptuous, at other times austere, food is one of life's perennially fascinating aspects.

For the practitioners of the visual arts, cooking is refreshment of the spirit, the epicurean's entertainment. Nadine Haim's book is the perfect illustration of that idea. As a modest monument to the pleasures of the kitchen, it delights the eye no less than the palate. It's a showcase of good food, to what remains in all of us a child's zest for treats.

There is a portrait of Nadine which shows her with a constellation of paintings revolving around her, paintings which she has nurtured and has helped send forth into the world. It is a perceptive image, and utterly true: Nadine Haim has a special gift for discovering and launching artists of talent. So it is true with this book of hers as well, conceived and carried through with that clearness of eye and intelligence so uniquely hers.

JEAN PAGET

OPPOSITE:
Claudio Bravo. *Pumpkin.* 1979. Pastel, 16⅛ × 21⅝″. Private collection

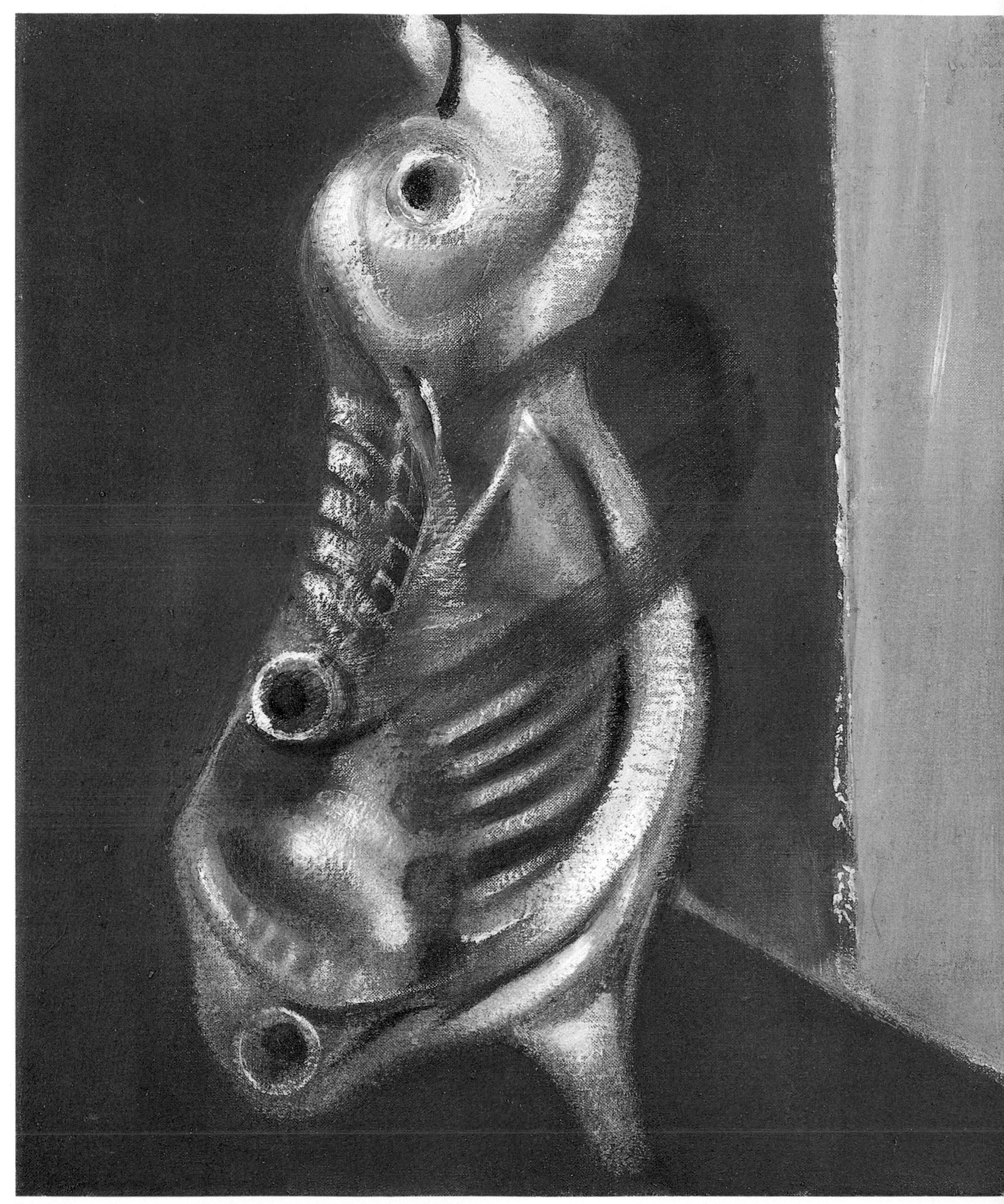

Francis Bacon. *Side of Beef*. 1978. Oil on canvas, 14 × 12″. Private collection

FRANCIS BACON

Born 1909, Ireland

To be one of Francis Bacon's friends is a privilege, because for him friendship is something that grows over the years. Moreover, when it comes to food, friendship becomes a schooling of epicurean sensations. I recall a memorable evening of bistro-hopping that ended up at Sonia Orwell's in the Rue d'Assas, where we decided to test the two recipes proposed here. I listened to Francis Bacon talk about the correct proportions required for syllabub and, with an apothecary's precision, weigh the respective advantages of the lamb kidneys he prefers with the beef kidneys, which are traditional in steak and kidney pie. After a free-for-all of pros and cons we reached a truce, which resulted in the final form of the recipes offered here.

STEAK AND KIDNEY PIE

2 pounds beef (rump steak, top quality)
5 lamb kidneys
3 onions
Salt and pepper
¼ pound kidney fat
3½ cups flour
¼ pound mushrooms, sliced
1 tablespoon chopped parsley
¼ teaspoon thyme

Remove the fat from the beef and kidneys, and set aside. Slice the kidneys into pieces and the rump steak into cubes. Peel the onions and chop them fine. Salt and pepper the meat. Dust the kidneys and beef with flour.

Make a pie dough by mixing the flour with the kidney fat and a little water. Let the dough rest for 1 hour.

In a medium-size skillet, cook the onions, mushrooms, parsley, and thyme for 3 to 4 minutes. Transfer to a bowl and mix well with the meat.

Roll out enough dough to line an earthenware dish; allow extra dough for extending just beyond the rim. Add the meat and onion mixture to the dish.

Roll out another sheet of dough, lay it over the top, and seal the edges, making a rolled rim all around the edge.

Set in a bain-marie and cook for 30 minutes in a 350° oven. Remove from bain-marie, and continue cooking another 30 minutes.

SYLLABUB

8 macaroons
Juice of 2 lemons
3 tablespoons sugar
½ teaspoon lemon zest
2 tablespoons sherry
Pinch of cinnamon
2 cups whipping cream

Crumble the macaroons into champagne glasses. In a well-chilled bowl mix the lemon juice, sugar, lemon zest, sherry, and cinnamon. Stir until the sugar melts. Add the cream and whip just until it holds its shape.

Pour the lemon and cream mixture over the macaroons and chill 3 hours. Makes 4 servings

WILLIAM BAILEY

Born 1930, United States

The meticulous care that William Bailey brings to everything he does makes this gouache a recipe that speaks for itself, with no need of instructions. One's appetite is stimulated just looking at this rendering of eggs and mortadella. A dash of salt, a sprinkling of pepper: you can already smell the sizzling eggs. You may even be tempted to eat the frying pan as well. . . . How can anyone say, after having savored this picture, that Americans are naïve when it comes to cooking? For William Bailey, a man with a cultivated palate, what we see here is no more than a simple, everyday breakfast.

EGGS AND MORTADELLA

(an Italo-Australian dish)

2 teaspoons oil
1 thin slice mortadella
2 eggs
Salt, pepper
Bread

Heat a little oil in a frying pan and brown the mortadella until it is crisp.

Break the eggs over the meat and turn down the heat. When the whites have set, carefully fold the mortadella over the eggs. Add salt and pepper and cook no more than another minute. Serve immediately with fresh bread or toast. Makes 1 serving

OPPOSITE:
William Bailey. *Eggs and Mortadella*. 1977. Gouache, 9 × 12¼″. Private collection

GÉRARD BARTHÉLÉMY

Born 1938, France

"I made this watercolor for you, dear Nadine, in our kitchen close to my studio, from which, thanks to the talent of my wife, Hélène, a true cordon bleu, *come delicious smells and subtler perfumes. It is where Courbet's saying often recurs to me that 'what counts before painting a picture is your appetite.' I will long remember the first time you came to dinner with us. For us you were an important person who represented 'the gallery,' and we were intimidated by you. We had taken pains over the menu, worked out the lighting. Everything was put in perfect order. Hélène had specially prepared potatoes* à la Périgord.

"At the time we owned a monkey, Joli Coeur. He gave you an exceptional welcome . . . by bombarding you with potatoes. The kitchen was turned into a veritable battlefield. Happily, you had the wit to find it amusing. So did we, and we became friends.

"In memory of that day here are three potatoes, because ever since then you have been part of our life, just as potatoes are part of our daily fare."

Gérard Barthélémy. *Hélène's Kitchen*. 1977. Watercolor, 20⅛ × 26". Private collection

STUFFED POTATOES

(a late-nineteenth-century recipe)

8 large potatoes
2 shallots, peeled
A handful of parsley
A handful of chives
¼ pound sliced bacon
2 tablespoons butter
Salt, pepper

Peel the potatoes and slice in half lengthwise. Scoop the potatoes out with a knife or spoon, taking care to leave the potato shell intact. Steam-cook the pulp and set aside.

Chop the shallots, parsley, chives, and bacon; mix well with the butter and salt and pepper. Blend with the steamed potato pulp, and stuff the potato halves with this mixture. Place them in a buttered shallow baking dish, dot with butter, and bake in a 350° oven for about 45 minutes. Makes 8 servings

BEEFSTEAK PÉRIGORD-STYLE

1 large shallot
¼ cup vinegar
¼ cup water
2 sticks butter
Salt, pepper
2 to 4 beefsteaks, grilled

Simmer the shallot in a saucepan with the vinegar and water until the liquid is completely reduced. Transfer to a double-boiler and add the butter in bits, stirring all the time as though preparing a mayonnaise. The sauce should be thick and creamy. Add salt and pepper. Serve alongside the grilled beefsteaks. Makes 2 to 4 servings

FISH AU GRATIN

1 quart mussels
2 pounds hake, fresh cod, or pollack (bluefish)
Court bouillon
Equal parts flour and butter
Lemon juice
Chopped parsley
Salt, pepper
Bread crumbs

Scrub the mussels carefully. Briefly steam them, as though preparing mussels marinière; remove from the shells. Reserve the steaming liquid. Cook the fish in a court bouillon, shred it into flakes, and combine with the mussels. Make a béchamel sauce with the flour, butter, and the water from the mussels (eked out, if you wish, with a little of the court bouillon in which you cooked the fish). Remove from the heat and stir in the lemon juice and parsley. Mix the béchamel with the fish, salt very lightly, and add pepper. Transfer to an ovenproof dish, sprinkle with bread crumbs, and brown in the oven. Makes 4 to 6 servings

WHITE BEAN PLATTER

3 onions
A few carrots
1 small celery root
A few potatoes
½ cup olive oil
2 cloves garlic, chopped
1 teaspoon salt
Pepper
Juice of 1 lemon
1 tablespoon sugar
1 tablespoon tomato paste
2 cans white beans (or dried beans cooked in advance)
Chopped parsley

Peel and cut into small pieces the onions, carrots, celery root, and potatoes. Cook in a pressure cooker with half the olive oil until tender. Add the garlic, salt, pepper, lemon juice, sugar, tomato paste, and 1 to 2 glasses of water. Cook for 25 minutes in the pressure cooker or 1¼ hours in a regular pot.

Add the white beans and continue cooking for a few minutes. Turn off the heat and stir in the remainder of the olive oil.

Let cool for at least half an hour in the pot. Transfer to a serving dish and sprinkle with chopped parsley. Serve at room temperature. The flavor of this dish improves a day after it has been prepared. It keeps nicely for several days. Makes 8 servings

JACK BEAL

Born 1931, United States

"This menu is typical of Sunday dinners served to family and friends when I was a child growing up in Virginia. The grown-ups ate in the dining room, which was furnished with the best china, linen, silver, and crystal. The children rarely ate with the adults, but when we did it was a memorable occasion.

"Mint juleps preceded the meal, and were served on the front lawn or on the veranda. The party moved inside at the first hint of serving, although all courtesies were strictly observed. The table setting glistened, and was embellished with trays and dishes filled with pickles, relishes, deviled eggs, and sliced tomatoes, pitchers of water, and iced tea, which was the most popular beverage. Biscuits with thin slices of country ham would be served first; sometimes in the summer beaten biscuits would replace hot buttermilk biscuits. Most of the food was produced on our farm, and the hams were from our own pigs, and cured in our smokehouse near the vegetable garden.

"Deviled crabs, a special treat in summer, were often brought home by a family member who had been near the Chesapeake Bay. At other times of the year, the fish course might have been catfish, eel, or shad roe caught by my father from the nearby James River, or bay oysters served raw or stewed. Perhaps the most common main course was Southern-fried chicken, usually accompanied by whipped potatoes, cream gravy, and fresh green peas. Other favorites were Brunswick stew (a cornucopia from the game-bag and the garden, put up in canning jars and served all winter), pork chops, steak and chitterlings, stewed chicken and dumplings, and ham with red-eye gravy.

"Although some families might have been 'too proud' to eat greens and pone (or, at least, to serve them to guests), our family and friends liked them and other 'ordinary food' too much to care about public opinion. Side dishes at our house also included corn-on-the-cob, lima and butter beans, succotash, hominy, black-eyed peas and stewed tomatoes (always served together), stringbeans ("snaps"), and so forth. Memorable breads included popovers, spoonbread, batterbread, and Sally Lunn rolls. A short pause preceded the desserts, which I seem to remember best of all. Peach cobbler, made with fruit from our own orchard, was often served with homemade peach ice cream on top. Other pies and cobblers were made from whatever fruit was in season, or from pecans, mincemeat, or yams. In winter we often had plum pudding with hard sauce, angel food cake, seven-layer cake, or lemon magic pie.

"All these meals were prepared by my grandmother and her cook, with help from my mother and other family members, on and in a large wood-burning cast-iron range. The memory of that stove, and of those meals, warms me yet."

BUTTERMILK BISCUITS

6 cups all-purpose flour
3 tablespoons baking powder
1½ teaspoons baking soda
1 tablespoon salt
1½ sticks butter
2 to 2½ cups buttermilk

Preheat oven to 450°.

Sift together the flour, baking powder, baking soda, and salt into a bowl. Blend in the butter using a pastry blender or your fingertips until the mixture resembles coarse meal. Make a depression in the center and stir in the cold buttermilk all at once. Stir quickly, but not more than 30 seconds. Turn mixture out onto lightly floured board. Knead gently for about 30 seconds, making 8 to 10 folds as you go. Roll or pat into ½-inch thickness, taking care to handle the dough as little as possible. Cut the biscuits with a 2-inch-round cutter. (You may use leftover trimmings, although these biscuits will not be as light.) Bake on ungreased baking sheets until the tops are browned, about 12 to 15 minutes. Serve hot with butter and country ham or cheese. Makes 24 to 30 biscuits

GREENS

2 tablespoons crushed red pepper
½ to ¾ pound slab bacon (or 4 to 6 small smoked ham hocks)
1 small onion, peeled and chopped
1 pound turnip greens
2 pounds collards or kale
1 bunch watercress
1 pound spinach
1 pound mustard greens

Fill a large pot halfway with water. Add the red pepper, slab bacon, and onion. Boil gently for 1½ hours. Meanwhile, wash, trim, and slice the greens. Add the turnip greens and collards to the pot and cook for 20 minutes. Stir in the remaining greens and cook an additional 20 to 30 minutes until tender.

CORN PONE

1 tablespoon butter
¾ cup boiling water
1 cup white cornmeal
1 teaspoon salt

Melt the butter in a heavy skillet. Pour the boiling water over the cornmeal and salt in a mixing bowl, and blend. Stir in the melted butter, and blend thoroughly. Cool.

Form into patties about ¾-inch-thick and about 2 inches in diameter. Place in the skillet and bake for 45 minutes in a 450° oven, or until crisp. Serve with butter.

OPPOSITE:
Jack Beal. *Still Life*. n.d. Pastel, 11¾ × 9". Private collection

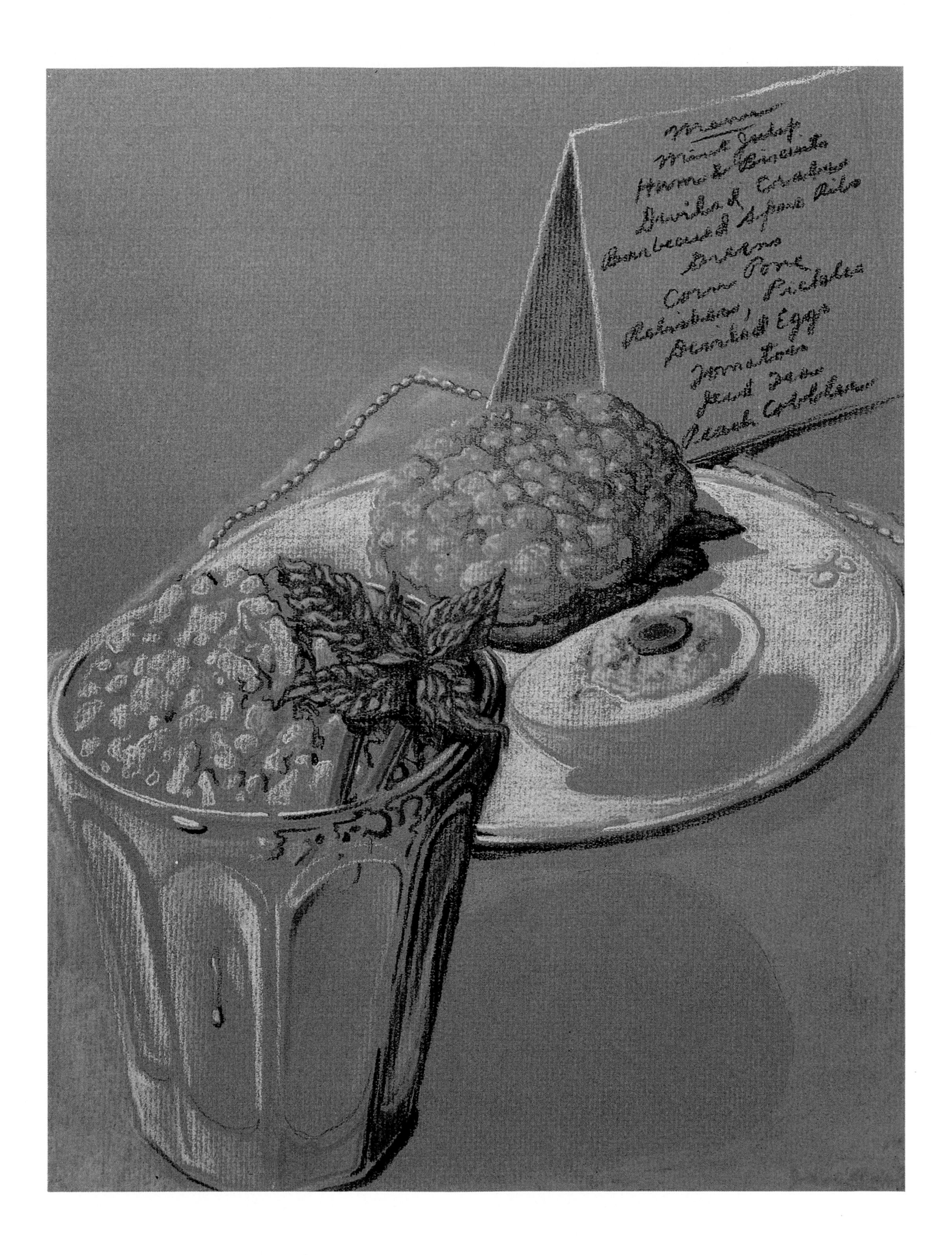
Menu
Mint Julep
Ham & Biscuits
Deviled Crabs
Barbecued Spare Ribs
Greens
Corn Pone
Relishes, Pickles
Deviled Eggs
Tomatoes
Iced Tea
Peach Cobbler

DEVILED CRAB

12 large crabs

Béchamel sauce
2 tablespoons butter
2 tablespoons flour
2 cups milk, heated

4 hard-boiled egg yolks, finely mashed
2 teaspoons prepared mustard
1 tablespoon chopped parsley
¼ teaspoon ground nutmeg
1 large pinch cayenne pepper
Salt
1 small onion
1 egg, beaten
1½ to 2 cups fresh bread crumbs

Boil 12 large crabs for 10 to 15 minutes, or steam them for 30 minutes. Drain and let cool. Break off the claws and separate the shells, taking care to preserve the upper shells; clean the shells. Remove and discard any spongy portions; reserve the clean crab meat.

Prepare the béchamel sauce. In a saucepan combine the butter and flour, and cook for 3 to 5 minutes. Whisk in the milk over low heat, and continue stirring until it is combined and the sauce has thickened. Remove from the heat. Stir the crabmeat into the sauce. Mix in the mashed egg yolks, mustard, parsley, nutmeg, cayenne, and salt to taste.

Rub the cleaned, reserved crab shells with a cut onion. Then pack them with the crab mixture. Brush with the beaten egg and sprinkle with the bread crumbs. Brown in a 400° oven. Serve hot.

BARBECUED SPARERIBS

Barbecue sauce
¼ cup chopped onion
Bacon drippings
¼ cup vegetable oil
½ cup water
1 tablespoon Worcestershire sauce
1 cup chili sauce
2 tablespoons wine vinegar
4 tablespoons brown sugar
2 cloves garlic, crushed
1 teaspoon pepper
1 teaspoon horseradish
1 teaspoon prepared mustard
1 large pinch paprika
Salt to taste

Spareribs (allow 1 pound per person)
1 onion
1 celery stalk
4 to 5 peppercorns
1 to 2 lemons, thinly sliced

Sauté the onion in bacon drippings. Then add the rest of the barbecue sauce ingredients, stir to combine, and simmer for 15 to 20 minutes. While the sauce is cooking, parboil the spareribs in water to cover with the onion, celery stalk, peppercorns, and a large pinch of salt. Cook for 20 minutes, then drain.

Preheat the oven to 375°. Place the ribs on a rack in a shallow pan and brush both sides with the sauce. Cover the ribs with the lemon slices. Bake 35 to 40 minutes, or until the ribs are crisp. Instead of cooking them in the oven, you may prefer to cook the ribs over a charcoal fire. If so, do not add the sauce until the last 15 to 20 minutes of cooking. Then baste continuously, adding the lemon slices at the very end of the cooking.

BAKED SPARERIBS

Cut the spareribs into sections of 3 to 4 ribs each, and salt and pepper lightly. Bake for 10 minutes in a fairly hot oven, about 375°; reduce heat to about 325°, and continue baking for 1 hour, or until the ribs are crisp. Baste every 8 minutes with the barbecue sauce, until about 5 minutes before the end of the cooking time.

DEEP-DISH PEACH PIE

Pastry dough, to form bottom and top crusts
8 to 10 fresh peaches
1 tablespoon butter
¾ cup brown sugar
¼ - ½ cup brandy
¼ teaspoon almond extract
Powdered sugar

Line a deep pie dish or shallow casserole with the dough. Peel, stone, and thinly slice the peaches, then add them to the dish. Cut the butter into small bits and distribute over the peaches. Gently stir in the brown sugar, brandy, and almond extract. For the top crust, cut dough into ½ -inch-wide strips and arrange over the peaches in a lattice pattern. Bake the pie for 10 to 15 minutes in a 450° oven, or just until the crust begins to brown. Lower temperature to 350°, and sprinkle with powdered sugar. Bake 5 to 10 minutes more, or until pastry is nicely browned.

MINT JULEP

2 cups sugar (for making simple syrup)
6 medium-size mint leaves plus 1 sprig
2½ ounces bourbon
Finely shaved ice
Powdered sugar

Chill a large glass or silver goblet in the freezer.

Prepare simple syrup by boiling 1 cup water with 2 cups sugar for 5 minutes. Cool.

In a large glass stir together 2 teaspoons of the simple syrup with the mint leaves, crushing the mint leaves to extract the flavor. Stir in 1½ ounces of the bourbon. Remove the chilled glass from the freezer and pack it with finely shaved ice. Strain the bourbon mixture and pour it over the ice. Stir vigorously. Add more shaved ice, the rest of the bourbon, and stir again, this time until the glass is frosted. Rinse a sprig of mint and dust it with the powdered sugar. Add the mint sprig to the drink and serve with a straw. Makes 1 serving

Botero 70

FERNANDO BOTERO

Born 1932, Colombia

Looking at a painting by Rembrandt, Velázquez, or Renoir immediately makes Botero want to bite off part of it and eat it—he has the great notion that painting is highly edible. Painting and cooking: two ways of expressing sensuality that, in Botero, are intimately linked. His voice takes on the same gluttonous tone when he speaks of the taste of a sancocho, *a fleshy face by Renoir, or the giant onions in his own paintings. His most unforgettable memory? That of a plain and simple fish that a beautiful black woman gave him to taste on a sandy beach in Colombia. The most insipid? The "painters' soup" he had to live on in New York whose recipe was passed on to him by an Italian painter down on his luck. It consisted of boiling two pounds of chicken offal—the parts Americans tend to throw away—together with an onion for a long time; you then reheated this thin broth whenever hunger got the best of you. For the cost of a dime, with water as the only other ingredient, an artist's survival was assured.*

AJIACO

(Pot-au-feu)

1 quart milk
1 quart water
3 pounds white chicken meat, cut into serving chunks
2 pounds potatoes, peeled and quartered
1 pound sweet potatoes, peeled and quartered
1 onion, peeled
2 leeks, chopped
Salt, pepper
1 pound beef ribs, cut into pieces
2 leaves of *guascas* (a Colombian aromatic herb)
1 teaspoon cumin
1 cup sour cream
1 cup capers
4 avocados
4 ears of corn, boiled and cut in half

Combine the milk and water in a pot, add the chicken, both kinds of potatoes, the onion, leeks, and salt and pepper. Cook for 1 hour. Remove the chicken and onion.

Next add the ribs, which have previously cooked in 1 pint of water. Add the *guascas* and cumin and cook for 15 minutes.

Serve the chicken, sour cream, capers, avocados, and corn separately on the side. Makes 8 servings

OPPOSITE:
Fernando Botero. *La estufa*. 1970. Oil on canvas, 74 × 59″. Private collection, U.S.A.

SANCOCHO

(a Colombian stew)

2 pounds beef chuck
2 pounds pork
2 onions, chopped
1 clove garlic, peeled and chopped
1 teaspoon cumin
Salt, pepper
4 large green bananas, peeled and cubed
1 pound yucas (Colombian potatoes), peeled and cubed
1 pound large potatoes, peeled and cut into chunks

For the sauce
2 tomatoes
1 onion, finely chopped
Juice of 1 lemon
1 tablespoon minced parsley
Cayenne pepper
1 red chili pepper
Salt, pepper

Cook the meat, onions, garlic, cumin, and salt and pepper in water. When the meat is cooked, add the bananas and yucas and continue cooking 20 minutes. Then add the potatoes and cook uncovered till tender.

Prepare the sauce. Crush the tomatoes in a pot, add the onion, lemon juice, parsley, cayenne pepper, and 1 tablespoon water, and combine well. Add the chili pepper and simmer 20 minutes. Season with salt and pepper. Serve with the meat. Makes 8 servings

COLOMBIAN SEBICHE

(Marinated Fish Salad)

2 pounds sole fillets
1 pint lemon juice
3 peppers, sliced julienne
2 onions, sliced in rings
2 cloves garlic, minced
1 red chili pepper
1 teaspoon salt
1 tablespoon olive oil

Cut the raw fish into small cubes, place in a salad bowl, and stir in half the lemon juice. In another bowl combine the peppers, onions, garlic, chili pepper, and salt, and cover with the remainder of the lemon juice. Marinate 30 minutes. Remove the chili pepper. Pour the marinade over the fish, stir well, and leave in the refrigerator for 1½ hours.

Before serving drizzle with olive oil.

CLAUDIO BRAVO

Born 1936, Chile

Claudio Bravo spends his life in a palace in Tangiers, in a decor where an abundance of animal skins lie scattered about the mosaic tile floors. His daily fare is no less luxurious.

When he gave a dinner there in my honor, I was surprised when at a late hour nothing had been served. I had forgotten that it was Ramadan, *the time of year when Moslems fast during the day, and eat after the sun has gone down. Although Claudio is not of that faith, he was respectful of the custom of the country that had welcomed him. Meanwhile though, I was beginning to wonder if he had forgotten dinner or was preparing some exceptional surprise.*

Finally at nightfall, and with a sign from Bravo, the house servants began to glide in, silent as shadows, bringing with them tray upon tray of food. Following the ritual soup with which one breaks the fast during Ramadan *came the most extraordinary inventions of the Italian, Chilean, and Moroccan cuisines. It made me wonder whether the art of eating isn't its own kind of religion.*

CARBONADA CRIOLLA

(Beef and Fruit Stew in a Pumpkin)

1 pumpkin, about 10 pounds
2 cloves garlic
2 large onions
1 green pepper
1 red pepper
1⅓ pounds stew beef
2 potatoes
2 sweet potatoes
3 tablespoons butter
3 tomatoes, quartered
1 tablespoon sugar
Salt, pepper
4 peaches, pitted and sliced
1 large can corn kernels, drained
1 cup beef bouillon

Cut the top off the pumpkin. Scoop out the seeds. Butter the lid and interior of the pumpkin. Cover the pumpkin with the lid and bake in a 375° oven until cooked but still firm, about 45 minutes.

Chop the garlic and onions, thinly slice the red and green peppers, cut the meat and all of the potatoes into 1-inch cubes.

In a large skillet melt the butter and add the garlic, onions, and peppers; cook about 5 minutes. Add the tomatoes and beef. Sprinkle with sugar, salt, and pepper and cook 15 minutes. Add both the potatoes, peaches, and corn kernels. Pour in the bouillon and simmer 40 minutes.

When well cooked, spoon the preparation into the baked pumpkin and cover with the lid. Serve in the pumpkin. Makes 6 servings

AGUSTIN CARDENAS

Born 1927, Cuba

It was at La Palette, the restaurant at the corner of Rue Jacques-Callot and Rue de Seine, where I asked Agustin for his recipe for Cuban-style lobster. He gave it to me, proffered with this sibylline warning: "Be careful. He who eats the sauce does not eat the flesh. And he who eats the flesh does not eat the sauce . . ."

ENCHILADO DE LANGOSTA

(Lobster in Sauce)

½ cup oil
4 large onions, roughly chopped
2 pounds tomatoes, cut into sixths
2 cloves garlic, peeled
4 medium-size lobsters
2 bay leaves
1 teaspoon oregano
Salt, pepper
2 cups dry white or red wine (Bordeaux)

Heat the oil in a pot and add the onions, the tomatoes, and the whole garlic cloves. Cook over low heat for 20 minutes.

Prepare the live lobsters: sever the spinal cord by inserting a knife at the joint where the head is joined to the body. Then cut up the lobsters into serving pieces; gently crush the claws. Add them to the pot, along with the bay leaves, oregano, salt, and pepper. When the lobsters turn red, pour in the wine and continue cooking until the alcohol has evaporated.

Shell the lobsters, set them on a plate, and dress with the hot sauce. Makes 4 to 6 servings

Agustin Cardenas. *Lobster*. 1978. Pastel, 9½ × 12⅝″.
Private collection. © ADAGP 1987

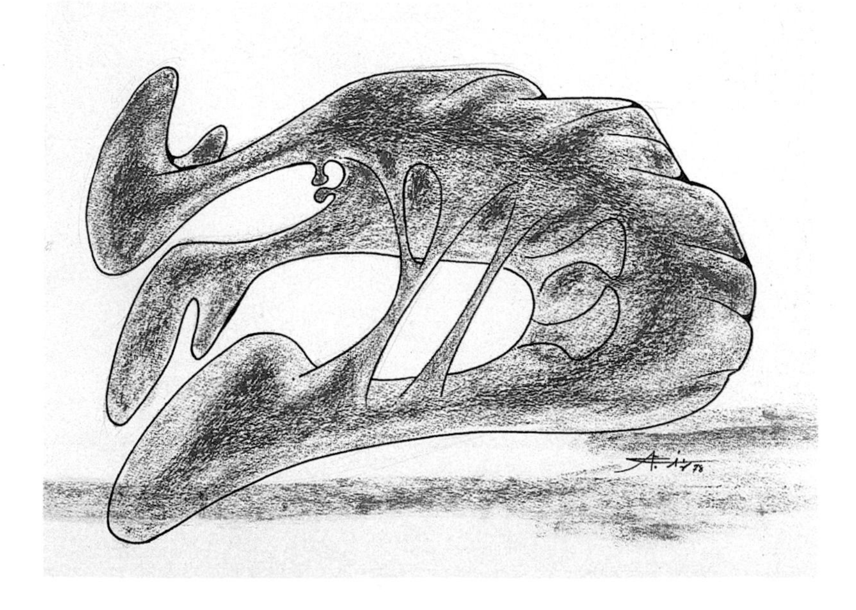

JUAN CARDENAS

Born 1939, Colombia

Juan Cardenas has an imperious way of looking at a person, although it is softened somewhat by the trace of a smile. Like most Latin Americans, Cardenas has a passion both for lime sherbet and for the fiesta, which probably also explains his attraction to disguises.

His pictures are often self-portraits in which he depicts himself variously as a violinist, as the poet Apollinaire after the war with a bandaged head, in nineteenth-century fashion in a redingote, or in a prelate's cape. It is as though he takes on different personae to escape from the reality of being a painter.

In Casquitos, *the painting which Cardenas contributed to this book, he gazes at us from the depths of a reflective globe. One imagines that from a great distance, a memory returns to him of a fête conjured up by a pensive magician. The enormous line in the foreground may be there to symbolize forbidden fruits to all we sinners. Just the same, does this mean we should condemn the bounties nature offers us?*

CEVICHE

2 pounds whole perch or bass *(róbalo)*
20 limes
Salt, pepper
Hot chili powder *(ají)*.
Minced garlic, as desired
5 onions

Remove the head, skin, and bones from the fish. Cut the fish into cubes. Put them in a bowl and cover with the juice of 14 limes, salt, pepper, and a little chili powder and minced garlic. Let marinate 2 hours.

Chop the onions, cover them with the juice of the remaining 6 limes, mix well, and pour over the fish. Cover or seal the dish and chill in the refrigerator for 1 hour before serving.

CASQUITOS DE LIMON

(Lime Shells)

12 large, juicy limes, preferably with their leaves
4 cups superfine sugar
½ pint heavy cream
4 egg whites
2 cups Drambuie or Strega

Cut the limes in half lengthwise. Remove some of the pulp and set aside to use in the syrup.

Cook the lime halves in a pressure cooker for 5 minutes. Change the water and repeat the process three or four times until the limes are very tender. Put them in a copper pot (this will help preserve their beautiful green color), add water to cover plus half of the sugar. Cover and boil gently for 10 minutes. Add the rest of the sugar little by little and more water as needed. When the peel becomes opaque, remove the limes from the pot and set aside to cool.

Pour the cooked syrup into a bowl and when cool mix it with the reserved lime pulp. Pour into an ice cream freezer or refrigerator tray. Meanwhile, whip the cream until peaks form. Beat the egg whites, then gently fold them into the cream. When the lime ice is almost set, stir in the whipped cream.

Fill the lime halves with the sherbet. Rejoin the lime halves. Pour Drambuie or Strega over each and garnish with the lime leaves. Return to the freezer for 30 minutes before serving.

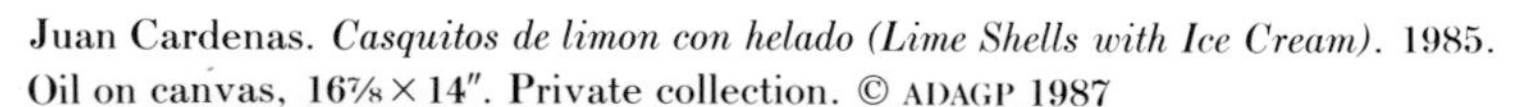

Juan Cardenas. *Casquitos de limon con helado (Lime Shells with Ice Cream).* 1985. Oil on canvas, 16⅞ × 14". Private collection. © ADAGP 1987

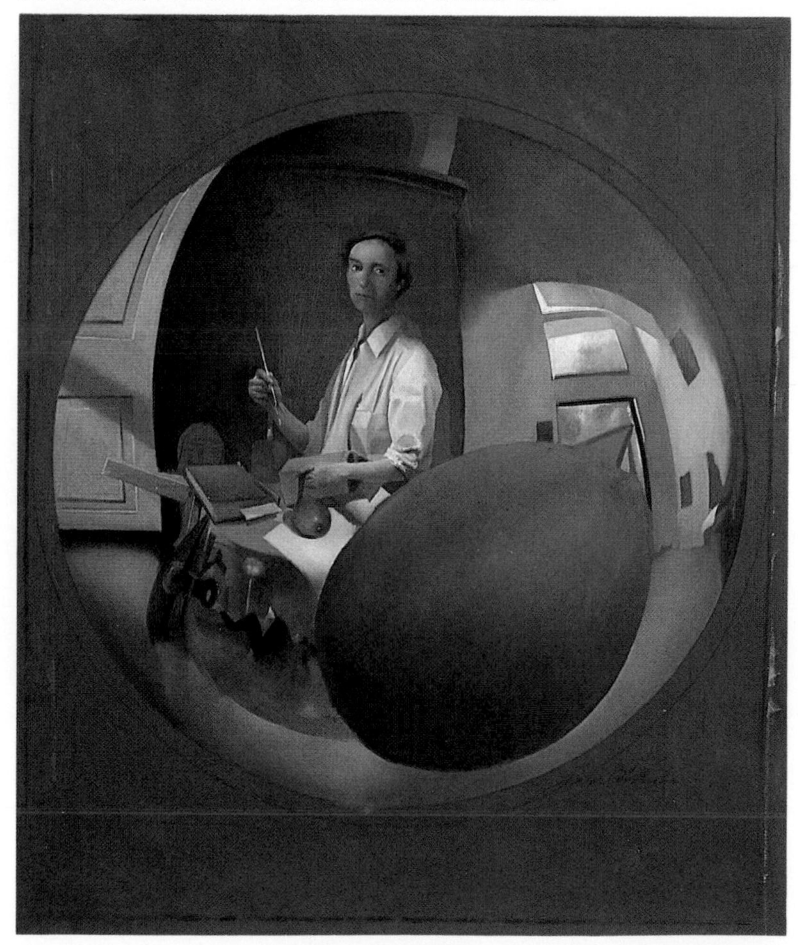

CÉSAR

Born 1921, France

"I have always loved to feed people, to go to the market and pick out my own fresh vegetables. I come from one of those Tuscan families who turn out a delicious meal with inexpensive ingredients. I always helped my mother in the kitchen. At first I only peeled foods, but by helping you do learn things. For example, now I can improvise a different dish of pasta day after day. Four olives, three onions, some cébettes, *a bit of basil, parsley—I can always turn out something fit to eat with whatever is on hand.*

"Tomatoes are a fruit of infinite uses. According to whether they come from Morocco or are grown locally, whether they are prepared peeled or left unpeeled, with the seeds or not, the sauce changes. And it can be cold, hot, simmered, or just barely cooked. The cook, like the artist, works with his materials. Like him, he has a technique which he invents with. Cooking is an art, both ephemeral and eternal. You have to know how to seize on the right things at the right moment, to reinvent, to catch the fleeting inspiration. The art of cooking is neither less nor more serious than sculpture."

ARTICHOKE OMELET

Artichoke hearts, thinly sliced
Peanut oil
Salt, pepper
White wine
3 eggs per person

Sauté the artichoke hearts in a little peanut oil. Add salt, pepper, and a little white wine. Simmer until the artichokes are tender. Remove the artichokes and set aside. Beat the eggs, add a little more oil to the sauté pan, and proceed in the usual manner for an omelet, adding the artichokes just before the omelet has set.

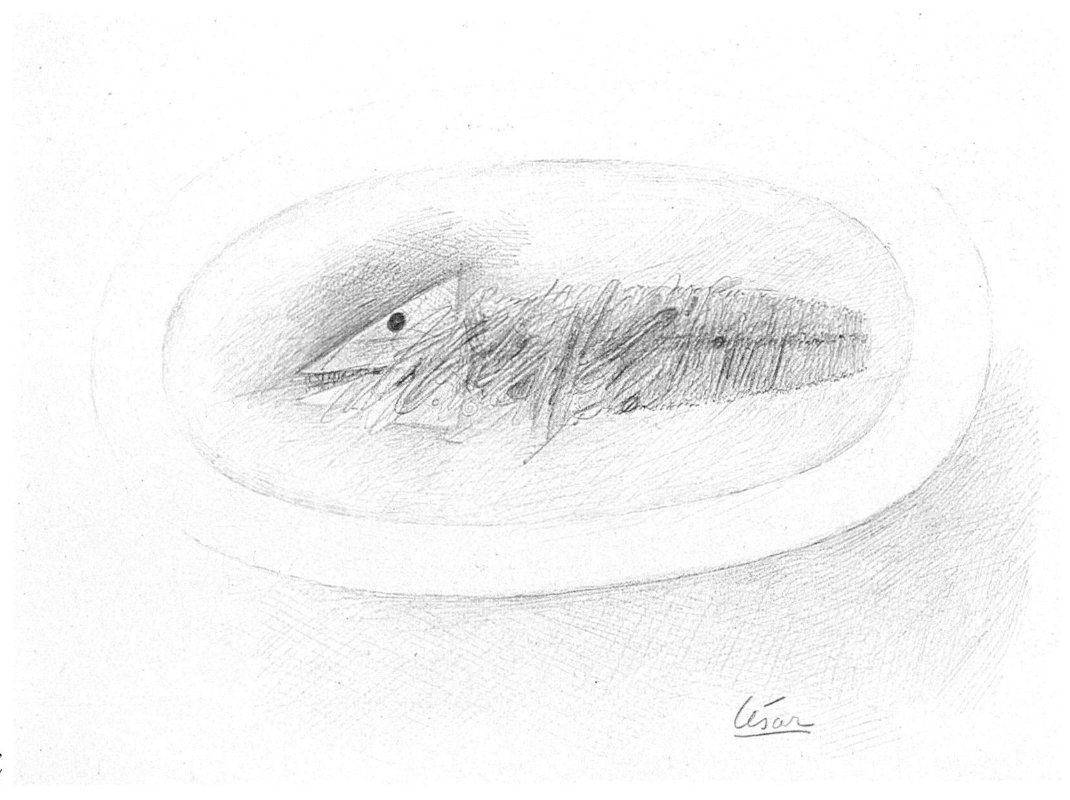

César. *Fish*. n.d. Pencil and colored pencils, 9 × 10½". Private collection. © SPADEM 1987

Salade pour 4 ou 6 pers.

après avoir enlevé les grosses feuilles
des artichauds violets et passé les
fonds au citron afin qu'ils ne noircis-
sent pas, couper ceux-ci en lamelles
fines. ajouter des fêves jeunes en en-
lever la peau si celles-ci est déja trop
épaisse - ajouter des olives noires dé-
noyautées, des oignons nouveaux coupés
fin et faire l'assaisonement avec
1 jus de citron sel poivre et huile
d'olives bazilic persil

A letter from César

SALAD FOR 4 OR 6 PERSONS

After having pulled the large leaves off purple artichokes and squeezed lemon juice on the hearts so they won't discolor, slice the hearts thinly. Add young fava beans, peeling them only if the skin is too thick. Add stoned black olives, thinly sliced scallions, and a dressing made with the juice of 1 lemon, salt, pepper, olive oil, basil, and parsley.

ROASTED SHOULDER OF LAMB

3 cloves garlic, minced
Thyme
Salt, pepper
1 shoulder of lamb, around 2½ pounds, boned
6 strips smoked bacon, finely sliced
1 cup beef stock or 1 bouillon cube, diluted
8 canned artichoke hearts, finely chopped
1 pound fresh pasta, preferably homemade

Mix the garlic with the thyme, salt, and pepper, and spread over the inside of the lamb. Roll up the meat, cover it with the sliced bacon, tie up the meat, and brown it in a 450° oven. Lower heat to 350° and roast the lamb. Halfway through the roasting, baste the lamb with the stock, at first only by tablespoonfuls. Eventually moisten the meat with the pan juices, then add the bouillon in small quantities so that the gravy does not become watery.

Separately, cook the artichoke hearts in a frying pan with a little of the stock and let simmer. Cook the pasta in abundant salted water.

When the meat is done, add the artichoke hearts to the roasting pan and serve with the pasta. Makes 4 servings

PASTA WITH ANCHOVIES

4 tablespoons peanut oil
16 ounces salted anchovies, rinsed well to remove salt
1 tablespoon capers
2 cloves garlic, peeled
2 pounds tomatoes
Basil, finely chopped
Parsley, finely chopped
Pepper
2 pounds homemade pasta
Parmesan cheese, grated

Heat the oil in a sauté pan. Add the anchovies and sauté with a spoon until they melt. Then add the capers, garlic, chopped tomatoes, and a little pepper.

Lower the heat and simmer until the sauce is reduced. Stir in the basil and parsley at the end of the cooking time.

Cook the pasta in a large amount of salted water. Drain, toss with the sauce, and serve with grated Parmesan cheese to taste. Makes 4 servings as a first course; 8 servings as a main course

PASTA WITH THYME SAUCE

Garlic
Olive oil
Fresh thyme
Pasta of your choice
Pepper

Count on about 1 clove garlic per person. Thinly slice the garlic. Cook in a skillet with hot oil and stir quickly until barely golden. Turn off the heat, and immediately crumble the thyme into the pan. Pour the sauce over just-cooked pasta, sprinkle with pepper, and mix well before serving.

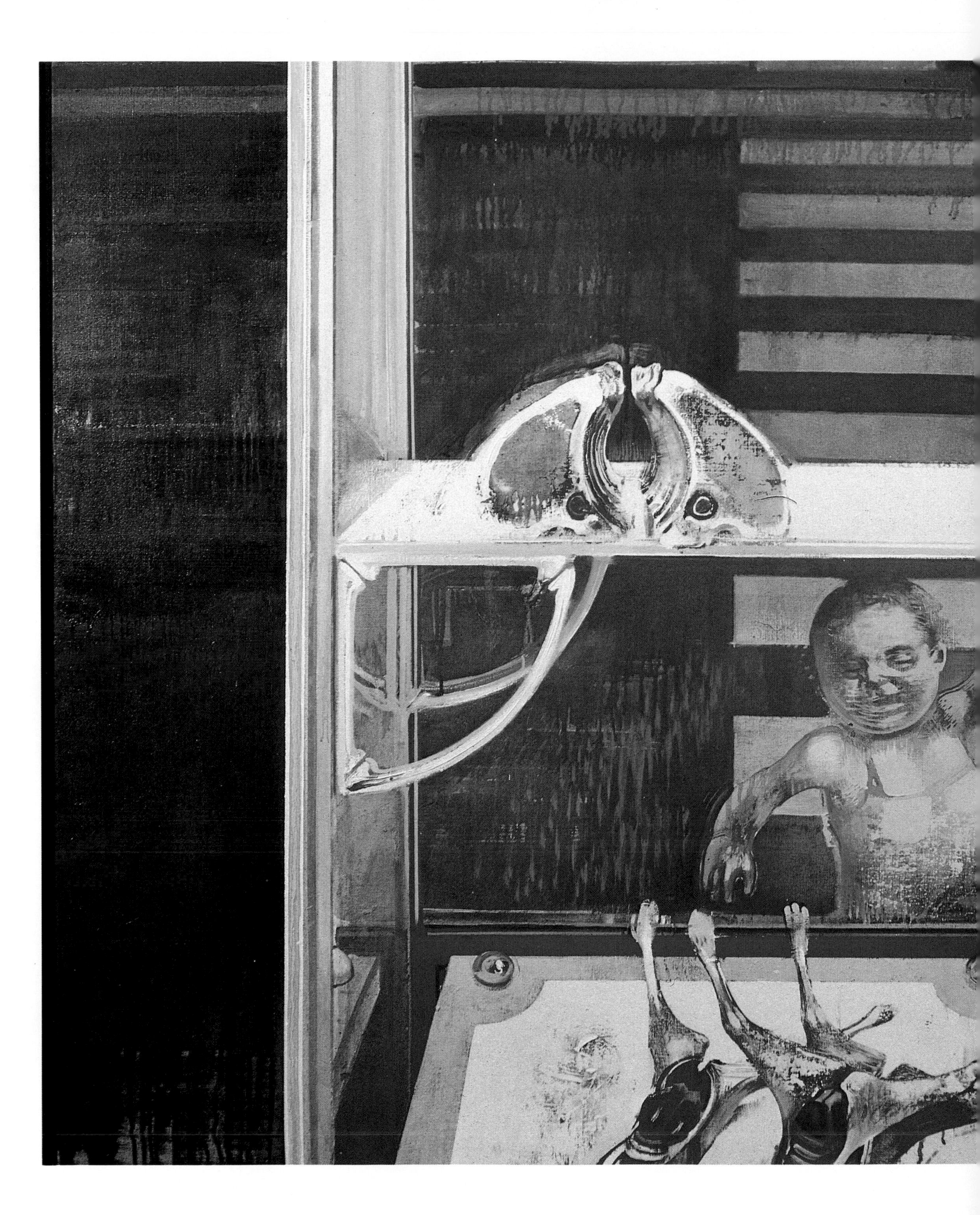

LEONARDO CREMONINI

Born 1925, Italy

"*My recipe shows what a glutton I am. Though the name I have given it is a kind of dedication to Nadine, there is certainly nothing about her that brings to mind a rabbit. But the 'agility' of a rabbit—*that *fits her. It is even, for me, one of her chief traits. In any case, I couldn't have created for her a plain rabbit cooked in a pot. Moreover, the name of my dish is based on something pretty funny. It was not until I actually settled in Paris that I learned how to spell the name of the celebrated Montmartre gathering place, Le Lapin Agile. In my Italian imagination the word* lapin *came to be associated with Watteau's painting of* Gilles, *thus* Le Lapin à Gilles. . . . *A restaurant decorated by Watteau perhaps? So whether it's* agile *or* à Gilles, *it is* à Nadine, *and to this day I think of the dish as connected with French painting.*"

"LAPIN AGILE" OR "À GILLES"

(Braised Rabbit)

2 saddles of rabbit
1 stick butter
½ pound smoked bacon, diced
2 bunches scallions, trimmed
1 to 1½ cups bouillon (or 1 cube diluted)
Salt, pepper
6 tablespoons flour
⅓ bottle dry red wine (Bordeaux)
2 pounds potatoes, peeled
1 small can mushrooms

Cut the rabbit into pieces, and brown them in the butter in a braising pan. Add the diced bacon and the scallions. Moisten with the bouillon and add salt and pepper. Cook over high heat for 15 minutes uncovered. Sprinkle lightly with flour and turn the pieces until they are well coated. Pour in the red wine and let simmer for 25 minutes. Before the rabbit is fully cooked, add the peeled potatoes and continue cooking for another 20 minutes. Before serving add the mushrooms and warm through. Makes 5 to 6 servings

PORK CHOPS WITH BACON

Brown pork chops on both sides in a skillet with very little butter plus cubed bacon. When the chops are cooked through, remove them from the skillet and set aside. Pour off the fat, reserving the bacon bits.

To prepare the sauce, sprinkle the bacon with a little flour, add a finely chopped shallot, moisten with 1 cup dry white wine, season with salt and pepper, and simmer for 10 minutes.

OPPOSITE:
Leonardo Cremonini. *Organized Senses (detail).* 1965–66. Oil on canvas, total dimensions 77 × 51″. Private collection, Modena, Italy.

TIBOR CSERNUS

Born 1927, Hungary

Tibor could have given me an authentic recipe for goulash, a dish which he takes quite seriously. For instance, if a waiter in a restaurant "slaloms" between the tables holding the dish hight in the air, Tibor sends it back to the kitchen: a true goulash is a soup, a very liquidy concoction that can only be carried from kitchen to table with due precaution. But he chose, instead, this recipe for an Easter cake. Even though he finds it a little heavy and sugary, the spiral of poppy seeds through folds of beaten white sugar delights his artist's eye. More especially, he may have chosen this because such cakes were the first sign of a holiday when he was a child in Hungary. Just before Easter or Christmas his mother threw herself into making them, and the whole house was sweet with the smell of pastry. In those days, the poppy seeds had to be ground and then mixed with honey to make a black paste. While you aren't likely to find a poppy seed grinder in your neighborhood today, Tibor has vivid memories of the one in his childhood home. It was painted blue, and its shape was exactly as those pictured in old Flemish still lifes.

When asked whether he finds a bond between painting and cooking, Tibor will tell you the story of the seventeenth-century Flemish painter Jordaens, to whom someone once remarked: "To see you paint such buxom and well-fleshed women one can tell that you love life and good eating." To which the artist replied, "Yes . . . the fact is, I adore the smell of turpentine!"

HUNGARIAN EASTER CAKE

Dough
2¼ cups flour
1½ sticks butter
1 pinch of salt
1 tablespoon sugar
2 egg yolks
½ ounce yeast
4 tablespoons milk, lukewarm

Filling
5 tablespoons milk
1¼ cups sugar
2 cups poppy seeds or chopped nuts
4 tablespoons butter plus 1 tablespoon melted butter
Raisins

Prepare the dough. Blend together the flour and butter. Make a well in the center and pour in the salt, sugar, egg yolks, and the yeast, which has been dissolved in the lukewarm milk. Knead the dough, then let rest for 30 minutes.

For the filling, warm the milk with the sugar. Add the poppy seeds or chopped nuts and stir a few minutes over low heat. Remove from the heat and stir in 4 tablespoons butter and the raisins.

Roll out the dough to make a thin rectangle. Spread the filling over it. Roll up as for a jelly roll and set on a buttered baking sheet. Let stand for 10 minutes. Brush with melted butter and bake in 400° oven for 30 to 40 minutes. Cool, then cut into slices about 1-inch thick. Makes 6 servings

OPPOSITE:
Tibor Csernus. *Poppy Seed Cake.* 1978. Oil on canvas, 15 × 17⅞". Private collection

GREGORIO CUARTAS

Born 1938, Colombia

As a child this Colombian, who at one time seriously considered entering a monastery, detested the beans that were his family's staple fare. Today, if it depended only on him, he would live on beans, lentils, and chickpeas. Now when he speaks of the food of his childhood there is enthusiasm in his voice. Pumpkins, which he delights in painting, were prepared by his mother in numerous ways: in soup, as a purée, in puddings, or to accompany braised meat. There were quinces, lemons, and onions that have inspired the many yellows in his paintings. The day before Christmas it was a tradition to slaughter a pig, and along with his eight brothers Cuartas would be sent off to give away portions to the needy in the neighborhood. Sometimes at Christmas there was even the luxury of a stewed chicken. There is no question that for Cuartas cooking is an art. Even marvelous is the pleasant memory of having prepared a meal after everyone has eaten.
It is a means of relaxation as well. Putting aside brushes and canvas, Cuartas will devote a whole day to the kitchen when friends are expected or just for his own pleasure. Even though he claims to have handed over the apron strings to his wife, as a lover of good fare he continues to haunt secondhand and antique shops for the utensils, molds, and casseroles that have had their part in culinary traditions through the centuries.

Gregorio Cuartas. *Onions*. 1978. Oil on canvas, 18⅞ × 26⅛". Private collection

Gregorio Cuartas. *Pumpkin*. 1977. Watercolor, 8 × 8″. Private collection

PUMPKIN PURÉE

1½ pounds pumpkin
Salt
1 teaspoon sugar
4 lumps of butter
5 tablespoons crème fraîche
Pepper

For garnish
Buttered croutons

Peel the pumpkin and cut into large cubes. Put in a large pot with just enough water to cover. Add salt and sprinkle with sugar. When the pulp is well cooked, drain it and pass through a food mill. Melt the butter and add it to the purée along with the cream. Mix with a wooden spoon. Add pepper to taste.

Serve with small croutons sautéed in butter. Makes 6 servings

BLACK BEANS À LA COLOMBIANA

1 pound black beans
1 good-sized piece of salt pork
Olive oil
2 onions, sliced
1 large carrot (or 2 medium or 3 small)
1 teaspoon cumin
2 or 3 bay leaves
Salt, pepper
A pinch of sugar
2 plantains, cut into small pieces
3 cloves garlic, finely minced

For garnish
Cooked rice
Chopped avocados
Sliced tomatoes
Chopped onions

Soak the beans in cold water the night before, changing the water two or three times.

The next day, cut the salt pork into cubes and fry them in olive oil in a large pot. Add the onions. When they are well browned add the beans and the carrot cut into cubes. Fill the pot with enough water to cover. Stir in the cumin, bay leaves, salt, pepper, and a pinch of sugar.

Cook over low heat for 4 hours, adding more water if necessary. Forty minutes before the end of cooking time, add the plantains to the pot. After another 15 minutes add the garlic.

Serve hot with rice, avocados, sliced tomatoes, and onions.

PIERRE ÉDOUARD

Born 1959, France

Pierre Édouard works in a studio which is terrifically cold in winter and like an inferno during the summer. As an antidote, he drinks quantities of tea, scalding hot or iced, depending on the season. This probably accounts for his well-balanced character.

INDIAN TEA

1 teaspoon Kisthi or Ceylon tea
1 cardamon seed
1 large pinch grated ginger
¼ stick cinnamon or ½ teaspoon powdered cinnamon
1 teaspoon superfine sugar (to taste)
1 cup water, hot or cold
1 cup milk, hot or cold

Put the tea in a teapot, pour the cup of water over it, and steep. Empty the liquid into a glass. Tie the cardamon seed, ginger, and cinnamon in some cheesecloth and steep the spice bag in the glass. Add the sugar and pour in the milk. Let steep for 15 minutes if you are drinking it hot, 25 minutes if cold.

OPPOSITE:
Pierre Édouard. *Man Drinking.* 1985. Pencil and charcoal, 18⅛ × 14⅛". Private collection. © ADAGP 1987

JEAN-MICHEL FOLON

Born 1934, Belgium

"This watercolor is a declaration of love for Italy. It brings together everything I love about that country. To begin with, there is the color Venetian red which Turner used. Watercolor, which is a lot of water and a little color, takes a long time to understand. It makes sense that it was discovered in Venice, a place so suited to the inner rhythm of watercolor. Another reason for loving Venice is The Dream of Saint Ursula, *Carpaccio's painting in the Accademia. It is something I go to see every time I am there. And finally, there is the* filetto alla carpaccio *invented by Harry's Bar. Those thin slices of raw meat are red when they are served, and then turn brown when a lemon is squeezed over them. It is the only dish that changes color while you eat it. It remains alive, and there is something magical about that metamorphosis. It's a little like watching a film. That reddish brown which brings to mind the old walls of Venice—of Tuscany no less—gives me the impression that I have the soul of Italy on my plate. And those white streaks among the reddish brown meat, they too are Italy. They are like the veins in marble, as in that from Carrara, but also like those on the sublime walls painted a faux marble by modest artisans, ordinary house painters who put all their art and so much love into those abstract paintings. In* Carpaccio *I have tried to paint the three slices of meat like the trompe l'oeil walls of Italy. The bowl symbolizes Bologna: I invented it thinking of Morandi who painted poor, simple dishes, poor bowls and plates. He made use of the most humble objects, everyday things used as traps for light which he transformed into architecture. His paintings have nothing to do with storytelling. His paintings are thoughts. Morandi painted the Italian soul as did Chekhov that of Russia.*

"But because the theme of this book is good food, I have also tried to evoke the flavors of Italy. For me it is the one country in the world where you eat the best, even in the simplest restaurant in a small village."

FILETTO ALLA CARPACCIO

Cut thin slices of very tender beef tenderloin (or the finest cut used for roasting) that has come from a young animal, no more than eighteen months old. Salt the slices and put them in the refrigerator for 10 to 15 minutes so they retain their color.

At Harry's Bar in Venice the carpaccio are seasoned with a mayonnaise diluted with a little cold bouillon (and perked up by a few drops of Worcestershire sauce).

At the Biffi Scala in Milan the most they add to the beef is some olive oil covered with thin shavings of Parmesan cheese.

Oddly enough, this dish, which has become a classic in Italy, isn't found in any cookbook.

OPPOSITE:
Jean-Michel Folon. *Carpaccio.* 1978. Watercolor, 11⁷⁄₁₆ × 8¾″. Private collection. © SPADEM 1987

Jean-Michel Folon and César.
Simple Sauce for Fresh Pasta. 1977.
Pencil and colored pencil, $9\frac{7}{8} \times 9\frac{7}{8}$".
Private collection. © SPADEM 1985

"If I have made spaghetti grow like curling hair around a head drawn by César, I did so as homage to Italy, and to the pasta that César has a divine knack of cooking. Perhaps this knack of his reflects what he puts into his cooking—generosity, a regard for friendship, and his unsatiable curiosity. But what he offers, along with whatever dish he turns out, César offers his conversation as well.

"Giacometti used to say, 'I would give all my work for a conversation.' César's conversation is like a long phrase flowing without interruption when he speaks about essential things: life, death, women, love, the sun. His tone is grave, but with a warmth that is moving, and always with the desire to see the positive side. César has the gift of introducing art into other people's lives. César helps one live."

SIMPLE SAUCE FOR HOMEMADE PASTA

½ cup olive oil
2 pounds tomatoes, peeled and cubed
1 or 2 cloves garlic (to taste)
10 basil leaves
Pepper or 1 small hot chili pepper
Salt
Grated Parmesan cheese

Put the olive oil, tomatoes, 1 or 2 cloves peeled garlic, basil, a good pinch of pepper (or the chili pepper), and salt in a skillet. Cook the sauce over low heat until slightly reduced, about 45 minutes.

Have plenty of grated Parmesan cheese on the table.

PIERO GUCCIONE

Born 1935, Italy

Like Bellini, the composer of Norma, *Piero Guccione is Sicilian. And as Guccione claims, there is a direct connection between pasta and that Druid priestess. The actor Angelo Musco, famous for his interpretations of Pirandello's plays (also Sicilian), had a cook who would regularly serve him spaghetti with tomato sauce, his favorite form of pasta. One day, though, she had the happy inspiration of adding to it sautéed eggplant. The marriage of the two flavors was so harmonious that Musco exclaimed, "It's as good as listening to* Norma!*" So to get the best out of those two pleasures serve this dish with Bellini as background music.*

SPAGHETTI ALLA NORMA O ALLA BELLINI

(a musical dish)

Spaghetti
Eggplant
Tomato sauce
Basil
Oil
Salt

Cook the spaghetti in an abundant amount of salted water. For each person prepare 5 or 6 slices of peeled and fried eggplant. Make a tomato sauce to which you add basil at the very end, and let it simmer a few minutes more. Drain the spaghetti and put it in a heated dish. Cover with the eggplant slices and sauce.

Piero Guccione. *Spaghetti alla Norma o alla Bellini.* 1977. Pastel, 7⅞ × 22¼". Private collection

EGGPLANT JEANNOISE

4 large eggplants
2 green peppers
2 onions
Salt, coarsely ground pepper
2 tablespoons olive oil
4 strips smoked bacon

Have your oven very hot (about 400°). Wash and dry the eggplants and peppers. Cut off the stem end of the eggplants and slice them in half lengthwise, taking care not to completely separate the halves (they should be like an open mussel).

Remove the stem and seeds from the peppers and slice them into thin strips. Peel and mince the onions. Stuff the inside of each eggplant with a layer of the onions and peppers—they will bulge a bit. Season with salt and pepper and drizzle some olive oil over each half. Add a strip of bacon to each stuffed eggplant. Bake 45 minutes. The skin should be slightly roasted. Makes 4 servings

CURRIED EGGS

(hors d'oeuvre or cocktail snack)

6 eggs
2 teaspoons curry powder
Salt, freshly ground pepper
2 tablespoons soft butter

Put the eggs into salted cold water and cook for 15 minutes. Run under cold water for a few minutes, then shell and slice them into halves. Carefully remove the yolks and combine them in a bowl with the curry powder, salt, and pepper, and mix well into a smooth paste. Add the butter and blend again. Using a teaspoon, fill each egg white with this paste and sprinkle with a bit of curry powder. Roquefort cheese can be substituted for the curry powder and tastes equally good in this recipe. Makes 6 servings

FRIED PARSLEY

3 large bunches curly parsley
Oil for deep frying

Wash the parsley and cut off the stems. Dry well with a cloth or paper towel. Heat the oil in a deep fryer. When it is hot, add the parsley and cook for a few minutes until it is crisp. Remove carefully with a slotted spoon. Not only an attractive garnish but delicious as well. Makes 4 to 5 servings

JEAN HÉLION

Born 1904, France

Like many painters, Hélion has always enjoyed cooking, especially improvising with whatever is on hand to feed friends who happen by the studio. He takes particular pleasure recalling fish he used to catch during the summers he spent in Belle-Ile, which he would later cook. Of all the odd, though successful, soups he has concocted on the spur of the moment, the most original combined an old chicken won in a village lottery with a spider crab; it was an outlandish match to begin with, and accompanied by other shellfish and wild herbs. But the recipe closest to his heart is a simple and easily made leek soup, which was the daily fare of his childhood.

Jean Hélion. *Homage to Reynault*. 1973. Colored pencil, 12⅝ × 17¾". © ADAGP 1987

CROISSANTS WITH ROQUEFORT

4 croissants
3 ounces Roquefort (about ½ cup crushed)
1 teaspoon butter

Split good-quality croissants lengthwise, but do not slice all the way through. Open them carefully.

Crush the Roquefort with a fork and blend it thoroughly with the butter. Spread the croissants with this mixture and reclose them.

Lay the croissants on a sheet of aluminum foil in a moderately hot oven (375°) and heat through for 10 to 15 minutes. Makes 4 servings

LEEK SOUP

2 leeks
1 large potato
Coarse salt
1 tablespoon thick cream
Day-old country-style bread

"This is the leek soup we ate every day of my Normandy childhood.

"For each serving, wash and peel 2 leeks. Slice the white and about one-third of the green part, slicing the tops into smaller pieces. Put in a pot along with 1½ quarts water, the peeled potato and the salt, and boil for 2 hours.

"Using individual earthenware bowls (ours were a dark purple Rouenware on the outside and crackled pale blue inside) or a large white tureen for everyone, we covered hearty slices of day-old country bread with a good tablespoonful of heavy cream per person and poured the hot soup over this. The soup should set a minute before eating. If, as is the best way, the soup is cooked in a cast-iron pot hung over a wood fire, about halfway into the cooking push the lid back a little to get a slightly smoky taste.

"The tradition in those days was that any leftover bread soaked in the soup was reheated the next day for the old folks' lunch, although the 'gourmets' did see to getting their share of it, too."

OPPOSITE:
Jean Hélion. *Leek Soup*. 1973. Oil on canvas, 36¼ × 23⅝". Private collection. © ADAGP 1987

strawberry cake
on a blue plate.

DAVID HOCKNEY

Born 1937, England

One day when David was in my office and we had finished with our business, he asked me to run out to the corner pastry shop and get some tarts. A sudden craving for sugar, no doubt. But before devouring the strawberry cake I had brought back he sent me out again, this time to buy colored pencils, whereupon he proceeded to immortalize the pastry on paper. He then ate the tart and insisted that I take down his favorite recipe for strawberry cake, which proved to be every bit as delicious as it looks in the portrait reproduced here.

STRAWBERRY CAKE

2 cups cake flour
2 tablespoons sugar
1 tablespoon plus 1 teaspoon baking powder
¼ teaspoon salt
½ teaspoon cream of tartar
4 tablespoons butter, well chilled
1 egg, well beaten
⅓ cup milk or light cream
1 cup heavy cream, chilled
1 pint strawberries, sliced and sugared, plus 6 to 8 whole strawberries
Strawberry preserves

Sift the dry ingredients into a large mixing bowl. Cut the butter into small pats and work it into the flour mixture, using either a pastry blender, two knives, or your fingertips. Do this quickly, and take care not to overhandle the dough; you should have a mixture resembling bread crumbs or large kernels. Then add the beaten egg all at once, and pour in the milk, stirring quickly and lightly to combine. When the dough barely holds together, it is ready.

Turn out onto a floured pastry board. Knead the dough about a half-dozen times, and pat into a rectangle. Cut the dough into squares and place in a well-greased pan or on a baking sheet. Bake in a preheated 425° oven for about 15 minutes, or until lightly golden.

Cool slightly, then carefully split the shortcakes in two, and lightly coat each half with softened butter. Whip the cream. Spread a small amount of whipped cream over each shortcake bottom and spoon on the sliced strawberries. Spread a thin film of strawberry preserves on each shortcake top. Crown the shortcake bottoms with jam-covered tops. Add more whipped cream and garnish each shortcake with a perfectly whole strawberry. Makes 6 large shortcakes or 8 medium size

OPPOSITE:
David Hockney. *Strawberry Cake on a Blue Plate.* 1978. Colored pencil, 13¾ × 16¾″. Private collection

GEORGES JEANCLOS

Born 1933, France

This is a dish for heroes—a Homeric recipe, straight out of the Iliad. *What is more, it's a labor of Hercules in which you shed every tear possible while slicing four pounds of onions per person . . . certainly a great dish, though Georges has been heard to mutter through his tears while preparing it the appalling thought: "What if my guests don't like onions?" Rather than attempting to draw this extraordinary dish, Georges chose to send me a portrait of a chef. It was a drawing of me because, he said, to really appreciate a menu it helps to know what its author looks like.*

HONEY CHICKEN

1 chicken
20 pounds large onions (4 pounds per person)
2 pounds honey
Salt, pepper

Peel and slice the onions and briefly cook them until they exude their juice. Lay the chicken on the bed of onions, add salt and pepper, and braise for about 50 minutes. Remove from the fire. Pour honey over the chicken to cover and place in a 400° oven for 10 minutes until caramelized. Makes 5 servings

Georges Jeanclos.
For Nadine, Our Chef. 1984.
Pencil drawing, $9\frac{1}{2} \times 8\frac{7}{8}''$.
Private collection

SIEGFRIED KLAPPER

Born 1918, West Africa

Siegfried Klapper, who is a model of sobriety and austerity, has lived at the foot of Mónt Ventoux in the Avignon region since leaving Germany. He only eats the fruits and vegetables that come from his own garden washed down with tea.

His way of life is almost monklike. "I came to the Midi," he told me, "to forget the cities in ruins and to forget the war, to find tranquillity. Which I scarcely manage to do," he added, "because my present home requires such a lot of work on the side: repairing my roof, taking care of my garden, my trees, chasing my dogs who run loose in the fields, building walls, sometimes stone by stone. . . ."

After such serious conversation, I felt reluctant to turn the talk to compotes and marmalades. But when I was served a sumptuous tea by Klapper on a terrace he had built sheltered from the wind, I found that hermits know everything there is to know about the good things in life that their retreats can offer.

APPLE PUDDING

½ cup raisins
¼ cup rum
5 apples
1 orange
½ cup red currant jelly
¾ cup superfine sugar

Plump the raisins in the rum, then sprinkle them on the bottom of a round oven dish. Slice the apples and arrange them over the raisins. Grate the orange rind over the apples. Make two or three layers of this mixture. Spread the apple slices fanwise, overlapping each other, for the top layer.

Beat the currant jelly with a fork in a bowl and spread it over the apples. Pour over 2 tablespoons of water and sprinkle the entire surface with sugar. Cook in a 350° oven for 25 to 30 minutes.

Serve either lukewarm or cold from the baking dish. Makes 6 servings

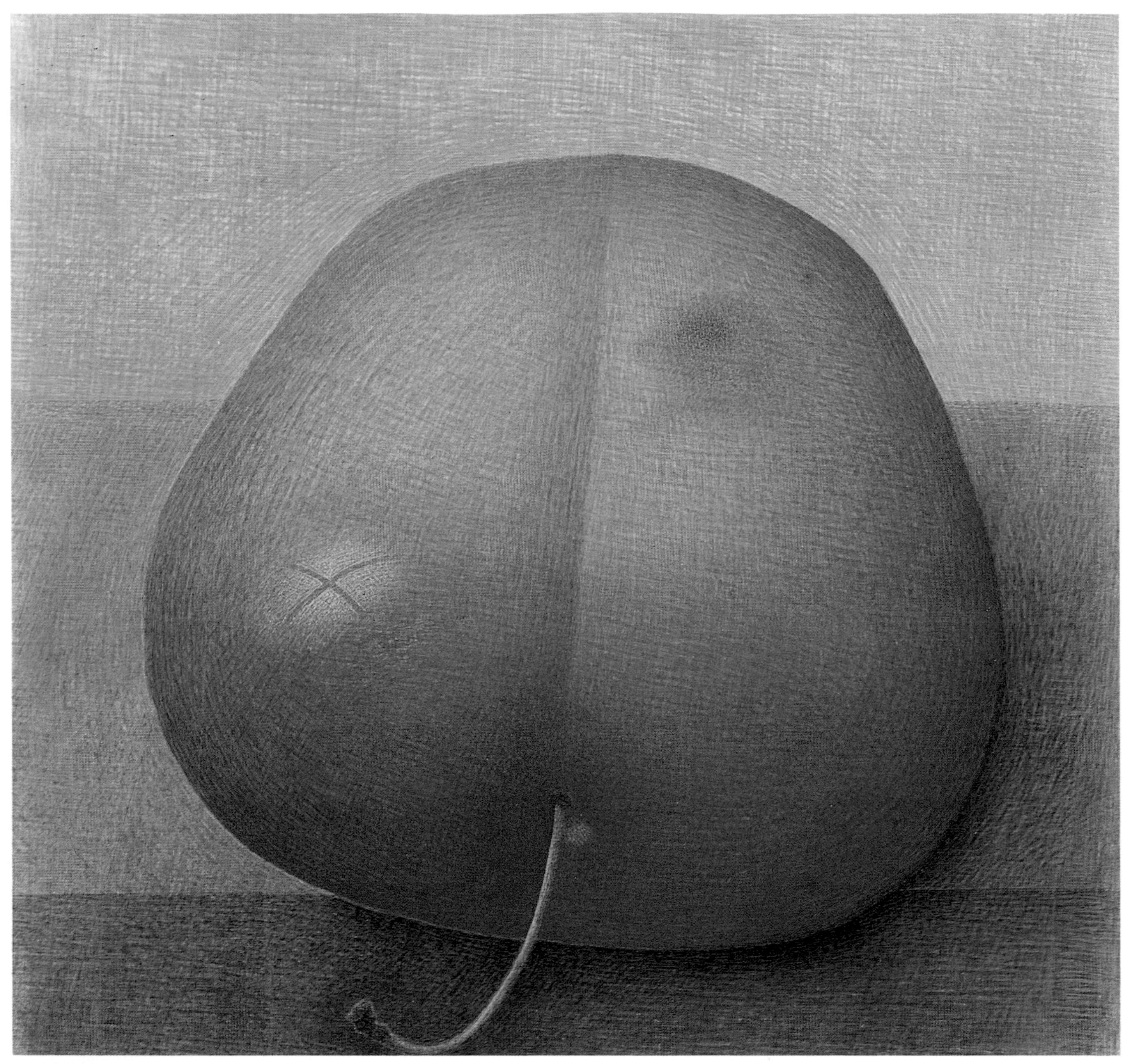

Siegfried Klapper. *Cherry*. 1978. Gouache, 6⁷⁄₁₆ × 6⅞". Galerie Claude Bernard, Paris

CHERRY COMPOTE

1¼ pounds cherries, pitted
⅔ cup red wine (Burgundy)
¾ cup superfine sugar
¼ cup kirsch
2 tablespoons red currant jelly
1 stick cinnamon

Combine the cherries, red wine, sugar, and cinnamon stick, and cook for 7 minutes. Remove the cherries. Reduce the syrup over low heat for another 8 minutes. Add the red currant jelly and the cooked cherries and heat the compote. Add the kirsch and flambé.
Makes 6 servings

YURI KUPER

Born 1940, U.S.S.R.

"When Nadine told me about her idea for a cookbook I racked my brain for everything I knew about cooking, eating, and the pleasures of the table. Since I haven't the slightest idea of how to cook anything except my morning cup of tea, I let my thoughts run to memories of the meals from my early years, their special smells and flavors. As a child, eating meant nothing to me except perhaps when my mother took me to a restaurant on a Sunday. I remember a delicious borscht with an island of sour cream in the middle. That meal was wonderful because I wasn't in school, my mother wasn't in her office, and we had time to tell each other about what we had done during the week. So it is that very special smell of meat and beets that comes back to me when I remember those Sundays. I thought maybe I could give that recipe, but it wouldn't be the same. Food has a different taste here in France. Salt, butter, oil, and cream all have the same names but are different from those that bring Russia to mind. And besides, cucumbers have a different smell in winter or in summer, bread is not as crisp when the weather turns damp, milk doesn't have the same taste in the city as in the country. What a pleasure to bite into a freshly picked apple! It tastes so much better than an apple you buy in the city.

"What I really like are dishes I can prepare with my own knife and fork, because there is nothing trompe-palate *or* trompe-palette *about them. They taste authentic."*

SWEET AND SOUR HERRING

4 salt herrings
2 red onions
3 ounces sweet and sour pickles
3 tablespoons peanut oil

Soak the herrings for 24 hours to remove the salt. Cut them in thin slices. Peel the onions and cut into small pieces. Chop the pickles. Combine with the peanut oil. To be eaten with buttered black bread and ice-cold vodka. Delicious.

CUCUMBER WITH COARSE SALT

(with an apéritif or as an hors d'oeuvre)

1 cucumber
1 teaspoon coarse salt

Wash the cucumber but do not peel it. Cut it in half lengthwise and rub the coarse salt into one of the halves. Let stand 10 minutes and then rub the salted half on the other.

SUMMER SALAD

5 new potatoes
1 egg
3 tomatoes
1 cucumber

Dressing
½ cup sour cream
Mustard
Salt, pepper

Boil the potatoes in their jackets. Boil the egg for 5 minutes. Wash the tomatoes and cucumber. Peel the potatoes. Slice the potatoes and tomatoes into quarters. Do not peel the cucumber. Slice into rounds. Slice the egg.

Mix the sour cream, mustard, salt, and pepper and pour over the salad.

TURYA

(to serve with an apéritif)

3 scallions
½ loaf whole wheat bread
2 tablespoons peanut oil
1 teaspoon coarse salt

Trim the scallions, slice into rounds, including the green stems. Remove the bread crust and slice the bread into small pieces; combine with the scallions. Add oil and salt and mix well.

OPPOSITE:
Yuri Kuper. *Country Lunch.* 1984. Mixed media, 31½ × 24¾″. Private collection. © SPADEM 1987

POUR NADINE

FRANÇOIS-XAVIER LALANNE

Born 1927, France

On a practical level it is fire that distinguishes us from animals, and it is at that precise point that cooking comes into play. Furthermore, the art of cookery distinguishes people from each other, differentiating them at the point between matters of need and sufficiency. Because if we need to feed ourselves to keep from dying of hunger, it suffices that we do not die of hunger over preferring good things to bad. Food as art resides essentially in the choice of materials, the order in which you dispose of them, and the way you transform them. This is true no matter what the recipe, because regardless of the methods you use, each has its own degree of excellence. In this domain, nothing can take the place of the cook's own sense and sensibility. As Poussin wrote to a friend, certain things cannot be learned—they depend as much on the painter himself, as on the materials. If a painter is to have full scope for his spirit and work, his materials must be of good quality, and capable of receiving the most excellent form.

What matters, therefore, is to bring one element to the point of perfection and, above all, never to stray beyond that. Cooking makes that possible. Just as the good smell that floats in the kitchen is no longer in the pot—and never will be so again—certainly it must have been there once.

RECIPE FOR A FISH STEW THAT IS DECIDEDLY NOT À LA DIEPPOISE

"Start with a pleasant, cool, flowing river chock-full of fish.[1] On a fine summer's day, take yourself fishing and catch two carp, a few medium-size catfish, some handsome perch, a two-foot pike, and two or three large rockfish. Of course a handful of crayfish would come in nicely, too—if you could ever find them au naturel which is more and more rare in these frozen-food times.

"In salted water which should not come to a boil (for by definition that is what court bouillon means), cook the base of the dish, your carp, until it becomes sticky to the touch. Put it through the strainer, but avoid using a grinder.

"Prepare a julienne of leeks and potatoes and add it to the broth, but undercook it slightly because its true flavor will develop with the last fish you add. Then, in this order, add large chunks of catfish, river perch,[2] and pike fillets which have been poached in advance.[3]

"Give the pepper mill a few turns, add a handful of parsley chopped by hand, and two good tablespoons of cream.

"Just before serving, throw in some rockfish fillets to tie it all together. The crayfish tails are optional. This is a dish of remarkable excellence: it all depends on the river you fished. The cook's hand is only to bring out the best in your raw ingredients."—François-Xavier Lalanne, Ury, March 8, 1985

[1]In his cookbook, Henri de Toulouse-Lautrec wrote, "Have on hand a glacier like the Wildstrubel or the Maïng, shoot a young chamois at an altitude of some 9,000 to 10,000 feet. . . . "
[2]Hold the perch by the tail and plunge them in boiling water for a few seconds. This is the only way to skin them before separating the fillets with a knife.
[3]When the pike is cooked, make a shallow longitudinal incision halfway between the dorsal line and the median line, then fold back the two lips of the incision. All the forked bones will be laid bare in a line, and you can remove them easily.

OPPOSITE:
François-Xavier Lalanne. *Landscape Fish.* 1976. Etching heightened by watercolor, 11 × 15½". © SPADEM 1987

DAVID LEVINE

Born 1926, United States

The only recipe that David Levine knows is that for Smeared Matzos, which was in his mother's cookbook. Like her, the dish comes from Lithuania. David assures me that this recipe helped the Allies win the last war because in Brooklyn, during those dark years, people organized charity bazaars to raise money for the American war effort, and the big seller was this homemade delicacy. All the women made food, but Mrs. Levine's matzos were widely appreciated and raised the most money for the cause. David was crazy about them. Salted, sugared, crumbled, mixed with cottage cheese to make a dessert—whatever form they took he wolfed them down; it would seem his mother was forever in the kitchen making him a new batch. By watching her at least he learned how to make this recipe.

GESHMEERTA

(Smeared matzos)

¼ cup flour
4 eggs, separated
¾ cup superfine sugar
2½ pounds cottage cheese
1 pint cream
1 tablespoon lemon juice
2 boxes plain matzos
1 cup milk
Cinnamon

Mix together the flour, beaten egg yolks, sugar, and cottage cheese. Then add the cream and lemon juice and mix well.

Beat the egg whites until almost stiff and fold into the mixture.

Moisten the matzos with milk but on one side only. Spread the mixture on the matzos almost to the edge. Sprinkle with cinnamon.

Lay the matzos on a cookie sheet and bake in a 350° oven for 15 to 20 minutes.

OPPOSITE:
David Levine. *Unlevined Bread.* 1987. Pen and ink, watercolor, 11 × 13¾″. Collection the artist

D. Levine 87

for Nadine with Love Richard
1 9 7 8

Richard Lindner. *For Nadine with Love.* 1978. Watercolor, 10⅝ × 13⅝″. Private collection

Like a prince in exile from Wagner's Germany, Richard Lindner was the perfect aristocrat and dandy. Born in Hamburg of Jewish parents, he was proud of his origins, although in another age he would have been named a baron by the King of Bavaria. Perhaps this gives some idea of how fascinating and intimidating he could be.

He reigned, impeccably, over a studio that looked more like an operating room. Though the decor was frigid, it had no effect on Richard Lindner's natural warmth. On my first visit there I bought a painting of a parrot whose reds, greens, blues, and yellows were sumptuous. It seemed almost a heraldic emblem, something between fable and myth, a mysterious bird, which, depending how it was viewed, also looked like the head of a woman. A few years later, Richard Lindner gave me the watercolor shown here for this book of a side of beef with an enigmatic face, and with colors like those of "my" parrot. I took it as evidence of a faithful friendship.

Lindner never ate at home, but almost always in a restaurant where he would order his favorite dish, goulash. A humble meal, but he drove there and back in his Rolls: a stately carriage for the Prince of Pop Art.

RICHARD LINDNER

1901–1978, Germany

SHOULDER OF BEEF WITH TOMATOES

1½ to 2 pounds shoulder of beef
1 tablespoon peanut oil
1 tablespoon butter
2 onions
1½ to 2 pounds tomatoes
Thyme
1 bay leaf
Salt, pepper
1 teaspoon sugar (optional)

For the marinade
1 onion
4 cloves
2 carrots
Bouquet garni
7 peppercorns
2 cups red wine

For the marinade, combine the onion quartered and stuck with cloves, sliced carrots, bouquet garni, peppercorns, and red wine. Add the beef and marinate for 12 hours in the refrigerator. After 6 hours turn the meat.

Drain the meat and pat dry. Let sit for 30 minutes until room temperature. Slice into large cubes. Lightly brown the meat in oil and butter. Remove from pan and set aside.

Chop the 2 onions and cook them in oil until soft. After 3 or 4 minutes add the tomatoes, thyme, bay leaf, salt, and pepper. Stir from time to time with a wooden spoon and cook uncovered over low heat for 15 to 20 minutes. If the sauce is too rich, sweeten with some sugar.

Add the meat to the pot. Simmer over very low heat, covered, for 10 to 15 minutes.

Serve with a crown of rice or with boiled potatoes. Makes 4 servings

PORK CHOPS WITH HORSERADISH

4 tablespoons butter
2 tablespoons flour
½ cup bouillon
Salt, pepper
6 tablespoons heavy cream
2 tablespoons horseradish
4 pork chops

In a small pot melt 3 tablespoons of butter over low heat. Add the flour, then moisten with the bouillon, and bring to boiling point, stirring. When the sauce has thickened, add salt and cream. Let simmer a few minutes more, then stir in the horseradish. Reduce the heat to a minimum.

Melt the remaining tablespoon of butter in a skillet and fry the chops 5 to 6 minutes on each side. Remove to a warm dish, sprinkle with salt and pepper, and pour the horseradish sauce over them. Makes 4 servings

CORN CRÊPES

For the batter
1½ cups sifted flour
3 eggs
1½ tablespoons oil
2 cups cold milk
Salt
2 tablespoons water
1½ sticks butter

For the filling
1 small can corn kernels
2 tablespoons melted butter
¼ cup milk
Salt, pepper

Sift the flour into a bowl and make a well and break the eggs into it. Add the oil, a little milk, and salt. Stir with a spoon or use a mixer until you have a smooth liquid. Beat the batter until air bubbles form. Add the rest of the milk a little at a time. The batter should be thin. Let sit 1 hour. If too thick, dilute with a little water.

Melt a little butter in a 5- to 7-inch skillet. For each crêpe, pour in 2 tablespoons batter. Tilt the pan so the batter spreads evenly. Cook until just lightly browned; flip with a spatula and brown the other side. Transfer the crêpes to a plate.

Drain the canned corn and spin it in a blender. Then add the melted butter, milk, salt, and pepper, and blend a little longer until you have a smooth purée. Put a tablespoon of the filling in the center of each cooked crêpe and roll up. Place the crêpes in a shallow buttered baking dish. Dot each crêpe with butter and reheat 20 minutes in a 350° oven. Makes 4 servings

GAZPACHO "COUCOU"

3 pounds ripe red tomatoes
1 green pepper
½ cucumber
½ onion
1 handful bread crumbs
2 tablespoons olive oil
Salt, pepper
1 tablespoon very good vinegar

Slice the tomatoes (do not peel) into chunks. Stem and seed the pepper. Peel the cucumber and onion and chop coarsely. Mix all the vegetables in a blender until they make a thick soup.

Dip the bread crumbs in the olive oil, squeeze, and mix into the soup with salt and pepper. Blend 2 or 3 minutes longer.

Chill in the refrigerator for 2 hours. Before serving add the vinegar and 3 or 4 ice cubes. Makes 4 servings

LUIS MARSANS

Born 1930, Spain

To invite Luis Marsans to a restaurant is a paradoxical undertaking. Whatever happens, and even in the most luxurious establishment, he will never touch anything other than vegetables and white cheese. He explains this choice to the maîtres d'hôtel with such subtlety that they end up taking his frugality to be the sign of a superior gourmet. And they also end up feeling it their duty to serve the quintessence of the simplest vegetable or the most ordinary cheese. Marsans saves his enthusiasm for desserts, perhaps because he thinks of them all as still lifes. Although Marsans doesn't eat desserts, he does share in the pleasure of seeing them on his guest's plate. For him they become objects of meditation.

COFFEE ICE

6 eggs
1½ cups superfine sugar
2 cups milk
1 ounce coffee extract
½ pint cream, whipped

Separate the eggs. Add sugar to the yolks and blend. Bring the milk to a boil and stir the coffee extract into it. Let cool. When lukewarm, pour it over the egg yolk and sugar mixture. Whip, using a beater. Strain. Then stir the sauce over very low heat until you get a slightly thick cream that clings to a wooden spoon. Remove from heat and cool. Chill in the refrigerator for 2 hours. Serve in tall glasses with a topping of whipped cream. Makes 6 servings

ORANGE ICE

2 cups milk
1¼ cups sugar
Juice of 2 pounds of oranges
8 eggs
2 cups heavy cream

Boil the milk, skim it, and let cool. Make a syrup by melting the sugar with ¼ cup water. Add the orange juice.

Beat the eggs. Add the cream. Strain this creamy mixture and mix in the syrup. Keep in the freezer for 2 hours. Makes 6 servings

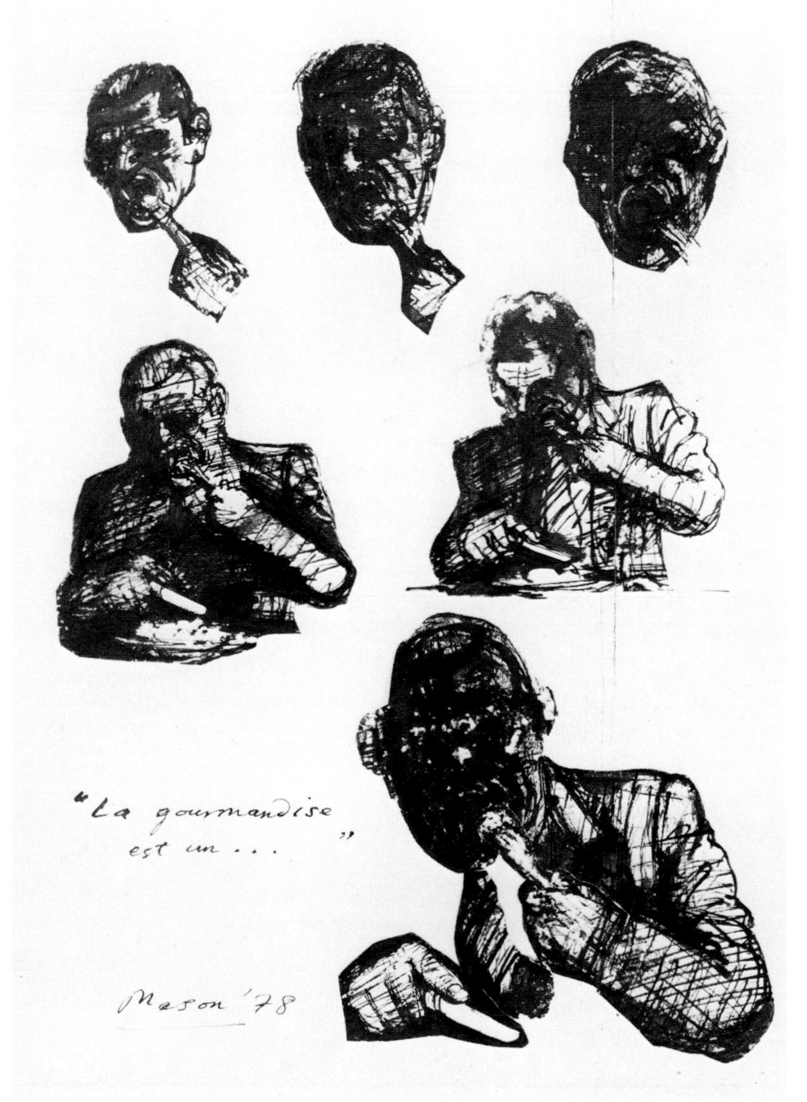

Raymond Mason. *La gourmandise est un . . . (Gluttony is a . . .).* 1978. India ink and collage, 14¾ × 11¾". Private collection. © SPADEM 1987

RAYMOND MASON

Born 1922, England

The English, as everyone knows, do not understand cooking. Or so some people say. It's an undeserved reputation, I think, because among them one finds great connoisseurs of wine, refined palates, knowledgeable gourmets. Raymond Mason has lived in France for forty years and has steeped himself in French culture. In doing so, he has not, alas, kept pace with his more enlightened countrymen. By his own admission he is more a gourmand than a gourmet. But with recipes like these he counts on our pardon.

POTATOES GOURMAND

8 large potatoes
1 cup light cream or milk
4 tablespoons butter
¼ cup grated cheese
Salt, pepper

Wash and dry the potatoes. Make a "cap" for the potatoes by slicing a slab of the potato. Bake the potatoes and caps for 20 minutes, then scoop out the pulp. Reserve the shells. Mix the pulp with cream or milk, butter, salt, and pepper. Stuff the potato shells with the purée. Sprinkle with grated cheese and top with a dab of butter. Replace the cap and bake in a 400° oven for 50 to 60 minutes. Five minutes before the end of baking, remove the cap to let the cheese brown. Makes 8 servings

CRAYFISH ON A SPIT

24 crayfish
½ pound lean bacon, sliced
6 bay leaves
Curry powder
Pepper, salt (very little)

Scald the crayfish for 5 minutes. Shell and remove the meat. On each skewer thread ½ bay leaf and a whole crayfish wrapped in a small strip of bacon that has been cut in half. Use four crayfish per skewer. Sprinkle with curry powder, pepper, and a little salt. Grill, turning so as to cook evenly. Makes 6 servings

MONICA MEIRA

Born 1949, England

Monica Meira makes one think of F. Scott Fitzgerald's heroines, fragile but bursting with vitality. And the fact is, she adores clothes of the twenties and has a whole wardrobe of them. It's easy to imagine her drinking pink martinis with the Great Gatsby.

During the year that Monica and her husband, the painter Juan Cardenas, spent in Paris they were delighted discovering Europe, but were homesick for the Colombian way of life where parties last till dawn and strange and magical things happen. Even in Paris, though, on the spur of the moment these two painters would put on disguises. Once when Monica and Juan were having dinner with me, they suddenly disappeared, returning minutes later in disguise. Out of an odd piece of cloth that lay about Monica had improvised the most astonishing toque, worthy of a Caroline Reboux. Juan had fitted himself out with garish false teeth that, with his lean face, gave him the look of a Don Quixote. For that moment, Paris seemed like a vast carnival, the air pungent with the scent of limes. . . .

PEPPERS WITH GARLIC

8 peppers, red and green
Vinegar
Salt, pepper
3 heads of garlic, broken into cloves and peeled
Olive oil

Grill the peppers to char the skin. Peel, and remove the seeds and stems. Slice fine. Cook in a saucepan with vinegar to cover. When the vinegar comes to a boil, remove the pepper slices, drain, and cool.

Pack the slices in a jar with salt and pepper and the garlic. Cover with olive oil and seal. Store in the refrigerator.

Serve as an entrée or to go with meat.

PAPAS CHORREADAS

(a native Colombian dish)

4 potatoes

Sauce
½ cup oil
2 tablespoons butter
2 onions or 4 shallots
4 tomatoes
Salt, pepper
½ cup grated cheese

Boil the potatoes in their jackets. To make the sauce, melt the butter and oil in a small pan and sauté the sliced onions or shallots until they become transparent. Add peeled tomatoes that have been chopped. Add salt and pepper and continue cooking for 5 minutes. Blend in the grated cheese. Chunk the potatoes and put in a serving dish. Stir in the sauce.

OPPOSITE:
Monica Meira. *Peppers with Garlic.* 1984. Watercolor, 14 × 11". Private collection

MANUEL H. MONPÓ

Born 1927, Spain

Monpó is the first to admit that he is a total zero in the kitchen. The most he aspires to making is his morning Nescafé. Though born in Valencia, he says he hasn't the slightest idea of how to prepare paella. But when it comes to appreciating that native dish he waxes poetical, convivial, lyrical—and proves himself an exacting gourmet. He will explain it's successful when every grain of cooked rice is separate from the others. Moreover, you can rely on him entirely to judge the quality of a meal and pay homage to creative cookery, and to create at the table a festive, warm, and cordial feeling.

Manuel H. Monpó. *Ambientes*. 1977. Colored pencils, pastel, ink, each sheet 12⅝ × 8⅞". Private collection

PAELLA "PERICA"

1 chicken, cut in pieces
1 pound pork ribs
10 to 12 small pork sausages
1½ tablespoons oil
½ cup lard
3 to 4 onions, grated
3 pounds peeled tomatoes, canned or fresh
3½ cups rice
2 quarts stock (or made with beef bouillon)
Salt, pepper
One 1-pound can green peas
1 pimiento, sliced
2 lemons, quartered

In a large frying pan sauté the chicken, ribs, and sausages in the oil and lard. Do not cook the sausages as long as the chicken and ribs. Melt the onions in a little oil in another pot. Add the tomatoes and let simmer for 40 minutes, stirring frequently. Transfer to a paella pan, add the rice; and cook over very low heat. Stir constantly for about 45 minutes until the rice has absorbed all the tomato sauce and become a little crackled. Lay the chicken pieces, ribs, and sausages over the rice. Pour over this the stock (double the quantity of rice) and add salt and pepper. Mix well. Over high heat stir the paella and shake the pan for 10 minutes, or as needed. Turn down the heat, add the peas, and arrange the pimiento slices in a star shape around the dish. Remove the pan from the fire and set it on a newspaper soaked in water or on a cloth bathed in vinegar. Cover and let sit 5 minutes before serving.

Serve with lemon quarters or squeeze a few drops of lemon juice on the rice, according to taste. If the rice is not dry enough, put it in a warm oven for 5 to 8 minutes. Makes 6 servings

NINGUNA JAULA CON
SILLAS CON RESPALDO
PÁJAROS — ESPERANDO
ALGUN TIEMPO PARA QUE
PASEN LIBRES.

OLOR A
Mejor una mesa redonda con
mantel de color limpio AGUA

COLOCAR LA MESA cerca
de una ventana. Detrás de la ventana
habrán árboles. Si no existiesen, unas
macetas con plantas y flores que se
compran en los mercados. (No son caras
y duran mucho tiempo)
CON SABOR A AZUL
DE CIELO

H. Mompó 77

Durante el día
o por la noche siempre
la luz dulce
No leer durante
la comida

LEJOS RUIDOS
SIN DEL TELEFONO
DE neveras
portazos
transistores
T.V.
y otros sinsabores locos.

ESTAR COMODAMENTE
SENTADO

H. Mompó 77

ARMANDO MORALES

Born 1927, Nicaragua

"There's every reason to believe there is a connection between cooking, good food, and painting. The proof is the way most painters—and musicians, too—appreciate a good meal, and which often leads them to turn their own hand to preparing one. This was partly because artists weren't flush with money (even truer in the past), so the only way they could eat properly was to do the cooking for themselves. It's also true that in the act of painting as in that of eating there is the same appeal to sensuality. The gestures called for in cooking are sometimes much like those made in the studio. And that, no doubt, is the origin of the expression, 'There is a lot of cookery in this painting.' "

Armando Morales. *Bodegón con arroz, frijoles, aceite sasso (Still Life with Rice, Beans, and Olive Oil).* 1985. Oil on panel, 7⅛ × 10⅝". Private collection

"MOORS AND CHRISTIANS"

(Beans and rice)

"Moors" (Beans)
½ pound red or black beans
1 medium onion, finely chopped
¼ green pepper, finely chopped
1 clove garlic
1 pinch oregano
1 bay leaf
Several small cubes of smoked bacon or salt pork
1 tablespoon good Italian olive oil
Salt to taste

"Christians" (Rice)
¾ cup long-grain rice
½ small onion, finely chopped
¼ small green pepper, finely chopped
Vegetable oil
Pinch of saffron
Salt

Wash the beans and soak in cold water overnight. Discard the water and put the beans in a large pot with approximately double the quantity of fresh water to beans. Add all the ingredients except for the salt and a teaspoonful each of the chopped onion and pepper. Cover, and cook over a very low fire, stirring from time to time, until the beans are ready—usually 4 to 6 hours. Add salt to taste and cook for another 5 minutes. Fry the remaining chopped onion and green pepper in a little vegetable oil until the onion is golden. Add the beans and some of the liquid and cook, stirring continuously, until the liquid has evaporated.

Wash the rice well and fry with the onion and green pepper until the rice is golden and translucent. Add the saffron, salt, and enough boiling water to cover the rice. Cover, and cook over low heat until the water is entirely absorbed, about 20 minutes.

When the rice and beans are ready, mix together and fry again until they are crisp and have a crumbly consistency. Makes 4 servings

"Moors and Christians" is a typical Latin American dish from the Caribbean, where it varies from one country to another. It is usually served with spare ribs or roast pork, and with fried green or ripe plantaines.

Morgan

RANDALL MORGAN

Born 1920, United States

It may be odd for this American from the Middle West to propose a dish using eggplant, a vegetable whose taste and very existence were unknown to him before settling in Italy. But perhaps this is a tribute to the Mediterranean countries that acquainted Randall Morgan with the smooth, oblong, purple, fleshy beauty and delights of this superb vegetable. Whether prepared with Parmesan cheese in the Italian manner, as moussaka done in Romania or Greece, as poor man's caviar Turkish-style, served with a chilled white wine or a beer, or savored on a shaded terrace overlooking the sea, for Randall Morgan eggplant is the symbol and feast of the Mediterranean summer.

MELANZANE A FUNGHETTO

(Eggplant, mushroom-style)

2 pounds eggplant
2 tablespoons salt
⅓ cup olive oil
3 cloves garlic
⅓ cup concentrated tomato purée
Pinch of oregano

Wash eggplant and trim stem; do not peel. Dice and put into a colander, sprinkle evenly with the salt. Let stand 30 minutes. Rinse well and pat dry, pressing out as much water as possible.

Heat ⅓ cup olive oil in a large heavy iron skillet and fry the garlic until almost golden; discard the garlic. Add the eggplant. Cook, stirring frequently, for about 10 to 12 minutes. Then clear a little circular space in the middle of the skillet and add the tomato purée, sprinkle with oregano and a pinch of salt and allow to simmer undisturbed for 1 minute; then blend with the eggplant. Cook for another 5 minutes, stirring frequently. Dish up and allow to cool to room temperature before serving.

OPPOSITE:
Randall Morgan. *Eggplants*. 1980. Mixed media, 9 7/16 × 11⅝″. Private collection. © ADAGP 1987

ZORAN MUSIC

Born 1909, Italy

Should young painters just starting out beware of the culinary art? Decide for yourself after reading Music's sad tale: "I had just exhibited my first works and two top-drawer art critics had taken note of them. I met them in the Piazza San Marco in Venice. There they flung themselves on me, drowning me in compliments. This went on until it was finally time to think about having lunch. Where else but at the Colombo? Yet I hadn't a cent in my pocket. The feast began and went on and on. Finally the waiters packed up and left, and only the owner remained. Then there was the bill, but my critics showed no intention of paying it. Finally they, too, took off, and it was only thanks to the owner's kindness that I was not turned over to the police. Even today I still have a soft spot for his polipi alla veneziana, *one of that famous restaurant's prize dishes."*

OCTOPUS VENETIAN-STYLE

Octopuses

For the court bouillon
4 to 6 quarts water, according to the number of octopuses
1 cup wine vinegar
1¾ pound onions, sliced
2 carrots
1 stalk celery
Bouquet garni
Parsley
1 heaping tablespoon salt
1 heaping tablespoon peppercorns
5 cloves
3 lemon slices

Sauce
Juice of 2 lemons
Olive oil
Chopped onion
Salt, pepper

Gently pound the octopuses with a rolling pin to tenderize them. Plunge the octopuses into just boiling court bouillon and cook for 45 minutes. Leave them in the court bouillon until you are ready to cut them into cubes and serve them.

Dress with a sauce of the lemons, oil, and seasonings.

OPPOSITE:
Zoran Music. *Poulpes à la vénitienne.* 1985. Gouache, 15¾ × 10⅞". Private collection. © ADAGP 1987

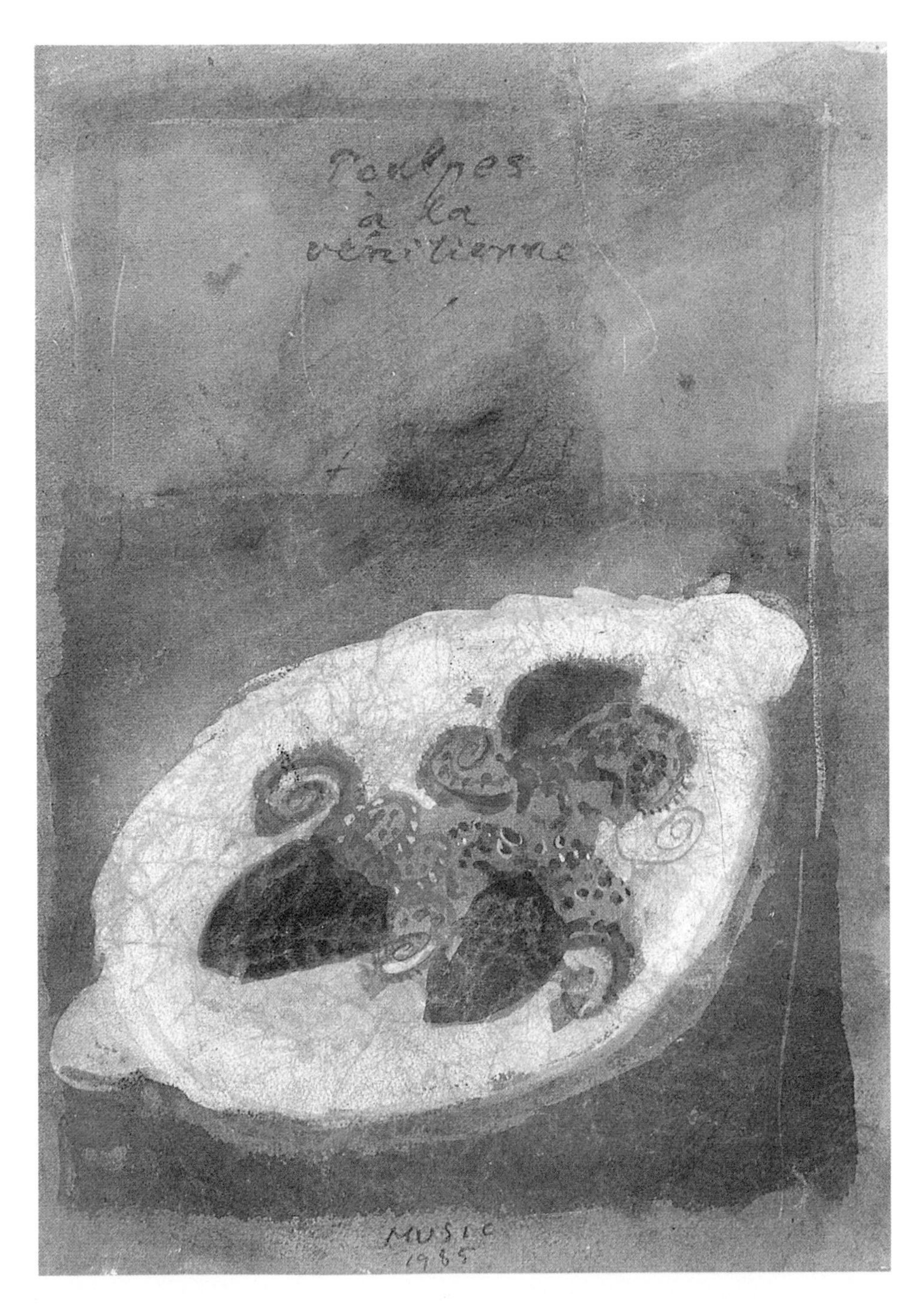
Poulpes
à la
vénitienne
MUSIC
1985

LOUIS PONS

Born 1927, France

"I was the oldest child in a family that lived humbly but still enjoyed good food during the sad years of the Occupation. One of the great points of disagreement with my father, a cook by profession, and which led to interminable arguments, was his claim that his métier be considered an art.

"All such allegations were met with a flat denial from me: I held exactly the opposite opinion. He would bring up the wise argument that one recognizes the artist *by the simplicity of his style, and that he should be judged not by his ability to concoct sophisticated sauces but by the way he boils an egg. Those battles belong to the dim past now. He has passed on, I am wiser with age. Now I consider cooking a genuine art worthy of the name. And after having recently eaten a hard-boiled egg prepared by my friend Nadine, I can say that she, too, is an* artist. *I no longer doubt that my father was every inch an* artist.

"As for whether I myself am one, the doubt still plagues me. . . ."

CAMEMBERT ON TOAST

1 Camembert, plus its wooden box
Bread
2 cloves garlic, peeled
1 tablespoon olive oil

Buy a Camembert worthy of being packaged in the classical round matchbox-wood case. Peel off and discard the paper wrapping. Put the cheese back in the box and place in a 400° oven. Meanwhile, prepare lightly toasted slices of bread and keep them warm. When the cheese begins to melt, remove from the oven. Rub the toast with the garlic cloves. Drizzle a bit of olive oil over the toast. Spread with the melting Camembert—and *bon appétit!*

Even better: use a Banon cheese, which is ewe cheese, wrapped in chestnut leaves.

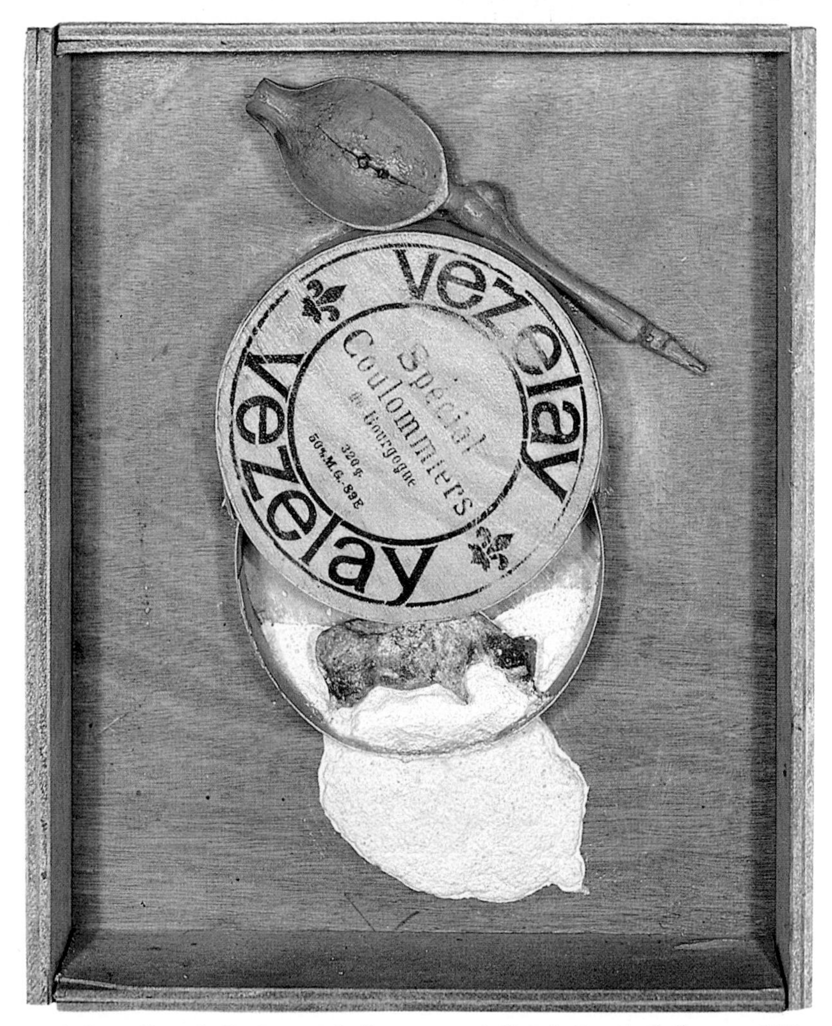

Louis Pons. *From the Producer to the Consumer.* n.d. Relief, 13 × 10¼". © ADAGP 1987

PEAR MERINGUE

3 tablespoons superfine sugar
Juice of 1 lemon
2 pounds William pears
3 tablespoons apricot marmalade
3 egg whites
3 tablespoons powdered sugar
3 ounces skinned and slivered almonds

Boil the sugar and lemon juice with 3 tablespoons of water to make a simple syrup. While it is cooking, peel the pears, cut them in quarters, and discard the seeds. Plunge them into the boiling syrup. Let them cook until the quarters become translucent. Carefully remove from the syrup without breaking them. Put them in a tall mold or a high-rimmed oval dish. Stir the apricot marmalade into the pear syrup and allow to thicken over low heat. Pour over the pears.

Beat the egg whites with the powdered sugar and a pinch of salt. When it has formed a meringue, spread over the pears. Sprinkle with chopped almonds and brown in the oven for 10 minutes. Serve warm.

ANDRÉ QUEFFURUS

Born 1939, France

When André gives a recipe, he never expresses himself in the prosaic manner of most cookbooks, so I hope he'll forgive me for translating his culinary poetry into kitchen prose. He takes it for granted that the chicken that laid the opal egg will be a virgin; that one does not simply scoop out the pear but bears through it with precision; that olives stuffed with pimientos taste better if you call them "la surprise du chat." *And that William pears stuffed with Roquefort are chiefly intended to disconcert his guests who are accustomed to a leisurely chat between the fruit and the cheese course, and find themselves suddenly with too much to say . . . or nothing at all.*

"And though I anoint myself with ointments of the Orient, you would embrace me only if I compelled you by some magnetic force."—Chopin to Titus

OPAL EGG

1 egg
Salt
10 grains black caviar
1 black Greek olive
1 hot red pimiento

Break an egg into a transparent bowl. Add a soupçon of salt, the caviar, and a black Greek olive stuffed with a red hot pimiento. Makes 1 serving

"ROUCOULADES" WITH MINT

2 goat cheeses (or ½ Montrachet)
A few sprigs fresh mint
4 veal cutlets, sliced thin
Butter

Mash the goat cheese with the chopped fresh mint. Spread the cutlets with this mixture and roll and tie them. Top with some butter, and bake until the veal is cooked through. Makes 4 servings

PEARS

6 tart William pears
2 ounces Roquefort cheese
¼ cup heavy cream
1 lemon, sliced

Core the pears and stuff with the mashed Roquefort. Nap a serving platter with the cream and arrange the pears. Decorate with lemon slices.

OPPOSITE:
André Queffurus. *Opal Egg*. 1977. Oil on canvas, 24 × 18⅛". Private collection

MATIAS QUETGLAS

Born 1946, Spain

"Here is a meal I recommend to artists short on cash. Day-old bread and eggs are both easy to come by and delicious. When you have to live in a modest rooming house whose owner forbids your doing any cooking in your room, you can always smuggle in a little electric stove and, with just bread and eggs, make yourself banquets worthy of the gods—the poorer ones, of course.

"In any case, I got by on this during my first years of struggle for glory."

ALIAIGUA AMB FIGUES

(Minorcan Soup with Figs)

2 very ripe large tomatoes
1 medium onion
1 small sweet green pepper
3 cloves garlic
Oil
Salt, mild pepper
Day-old bread, thinly sliced
12 fresh figs

In a soup pot combine the coarsely cut tomatoes, chopped onion, sweet pepper, and chopped garlic with a very little water and cook until the onion is tender. Add a little oil and simmer until the liquid is reduced. Add salt and pepper. Pour in 3 glasses of water; leave on the heat until the soup begins to bubble, but by no means let it boil.

Pour the soup over a slice of bread in each soup bowl. Peel the fresh figs and serve them with the soup. The quality of the bread and the sweetness of the figs make the dish special. Can be served cold. Makes 3 servings

EGGPLANT CIUDADELA-STYLE

2 pounds small eggplants
Olive oil
1 tomato
1 large onion
2 cloves garlic
1 green chili pepper
Bread crumbs (about ¼ cup)
Parsley
Salt, pepper

Remove the eggplant stems. Wash and dry the eggplants, and slice them in half. Fry the eggplants in hot oil for about 10 minutes. When they are soft, remove from pan, and scoop out the pulp without breaking the skin.

Peel the tomato, onion, and garlic and chop them coarsely with the chili pepper. Simmer in a frying pan with salt and pepper until any juice from the tomato has cooked off.

Mash the eggplant with a fork and mix it with 2 generous tablespoonfuls of the bread crumbs and some chopped parsley. Mix this with the tomato and onion preparation and stuff the eggplant shells with the mixture. Pour a little oil on each half and cover with bread crumbs. Transfer to an ovenproof dish and bake in a 350° oven for 30 to 40 minutes.

Variation: To the stuffing add ¼ pound finely chopped meat, 1 beaten egg, a small handful of bread soaked in milk, thyme, and diced pimiento.

Matias Quetglas. *Di Aliaigua con higos*. 1977. Watercolor, 14 × 12⅝". Private collection, Spain

CERDO CON BONIATO

(Pork with Rutabagas)

1 pound lean pork, cubed
Oil
1 pound rutabagas
Salt, pepper
Milk

Lightly brown the pork cubes in oil in an earthenware dish. Add salt. Remove from the heat and cover the meat with rutabagas peeled and cut into rounds ½- to ¾-inches thick. Add pepper. Cover with milk. Bake in a 350° oven until half the milk has cooked off. When done, the dish should look candied. Even better heated up the next day.

CUSCUSSÓ

(a Minorcan specialty, a kind of nougat)

A handful of raisins
⅔ cup vegetable shortening
¾ pound dry salt-free bread, crumbed
2½ cups superfine sugar
1½ cups almonds, peeled and chopped
1 small lemon, grated
1 scant teaspoon cinnamon

Plump the raisins in a little water; drain. Melt the shortening in an earthenware casserole.

In a bowl mix the crumbed bread, sugar, almonds, grated lemon peel, and cinnamon. Combine in the casserole with the raisins and melted shortening and stir over the heat for 7 to 8 minutes.

Pour this dough into a shallow rectangular mold or onto a jellyroll pan, patting into the shape of a large nougat.

Serve cold. Keeps well.

TORTADA

(a Minorcan dessert)

6 whole eggs
2 cups superfine sugar
2½ cups chopped almonds
Grated lemon peel
Cinnamon
4 egg whites
Candied cherries

Break the 6 whole eggs into a bowl with 1 cup of the sugar. Beat well. Then add the chopped almonds, grated lemon peel, cinnamon, and the remaining sugar. Beat a few more minutes. Separately, whip 4 egg whites and fold them into the mixture. Pour into a mold. Bake about 25 minutes in a 450° oven, then reduce the heat to 225° and continue baking another 25 minutes. Let cool, then remove from mold, and garnish the top with candied cherries. Makes 6 servings

EMPANADAS DE BROSSAT

(a Minorcan filled pastry)

For the dough
¾ ounce yeast
8½ cups flour
2 cups vegetable shortening

For the filling
1 quart buttermilk
1 pound sugar
4 eggs
Cinnamon
Lemon zest

Dissolve the yeast in a little lukewarm water. Add to the shortening and flour. Knead the dough well. Set aside to rise. To check whether the bread has risen, press the dough with your finger: if the depression remains, the dough is ready.

Combine the buttermilk, sugar, eggs, cinnamon, and lemon zest in a bowl with an electric beater.

When the dough has risen, flatten it with a rolling pin. Then cut out circles 3 inches or so in diameter using a scalloped dough cutter. On half of the circles lay an abundant tablespoonful of the buttermilk filling. On the other half make 4 to 6 thin slits with a pastry wheel. Fold over the filling and pinch the dough all around to seal.

Set aside for about 2 hours. Bake in a 400° oven until the crust is golden. Makes 12 servings

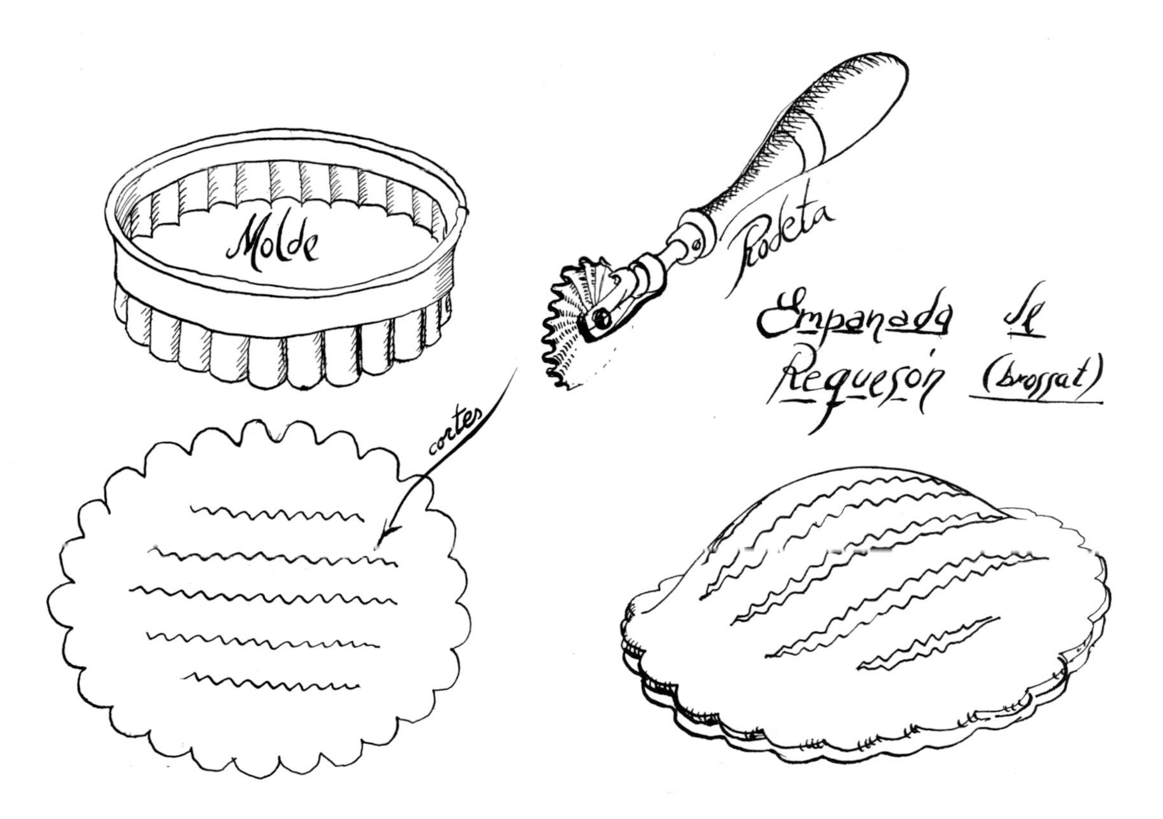

Matias Quetglas. *Empanada*. Sketch. Private collection

DANIEL QUINTERO

Born 1949, Spain

"Can one separate culinary pleasure and artistic realization? For my part I have arrived at a half-serious, half-humorous somewhat biological conception of the act of painting. I think climate has a decisive influence on the artist, even if less subtle, and agreeably human factors also have their part in bringing into being every work of art and also contributing to making it what it is. The food that nourishes the artist, like the color of the earth where he lives, gives him his personal palette, in that each country and its vegetation has its own particular color ranges.

"In France, for example, carrots, cabbages, and lettuces lend their colors to the works of Bonnard, Matisse, Vuillard. The colors of their canvases are as fresh as those of French kitchen gardens.

"The color of the austere soil of Spain, brown and gray and with accents of ocher and blood-red, is found again in Velázquez, Zurbarán, Murillo. You see it, too, in the hue of lentils and chick-peas, even if here and there is the green hue of olives.

"Great Britain is a country wet both inside and out—both because of its climate and that it imports wines from all over. Whence its watercolorists, its landscapes with mossy trees, the foliage Gainsborough painted. Even its green peas served at every meal. . . .

"Without ever having been in Italy, I can imagine that Titian must have known about saffron judging by the many golden tints in his canvases. The United States poses a special problem. The artists who inhabit that vast territory come from areas where the soil has nourished three generations, at the least. Today Americans have ended up with the self-service eatery and the orange plastic tray. Marcel Duchamp made off with the spoon and Andy Warhol contributed the tin can. Enormous canvases have been realized in absolute liberty. Streaks of color crisscross like ketchup on a hamburger. All of which must certainly give rise to and encourage a particular mode of expression. Tell me what you eat and I will tell you what you paint."

GARLIC BREAD

For 1½-pound French bread, approximately:
6 cloves garlic, chopped
Salt
¼ cup olive oil

Use day-old bread if you wish. Make 7 or 8 cuts in the loaf without cutting all the way through. Insert the chopped garlic, salt, and olive oil into each slice. Heat in the oven for 10 minutes.

Daniel Quintero. *Bread*. n.d. Dry point, 2½ × 11⅝″. Private collection

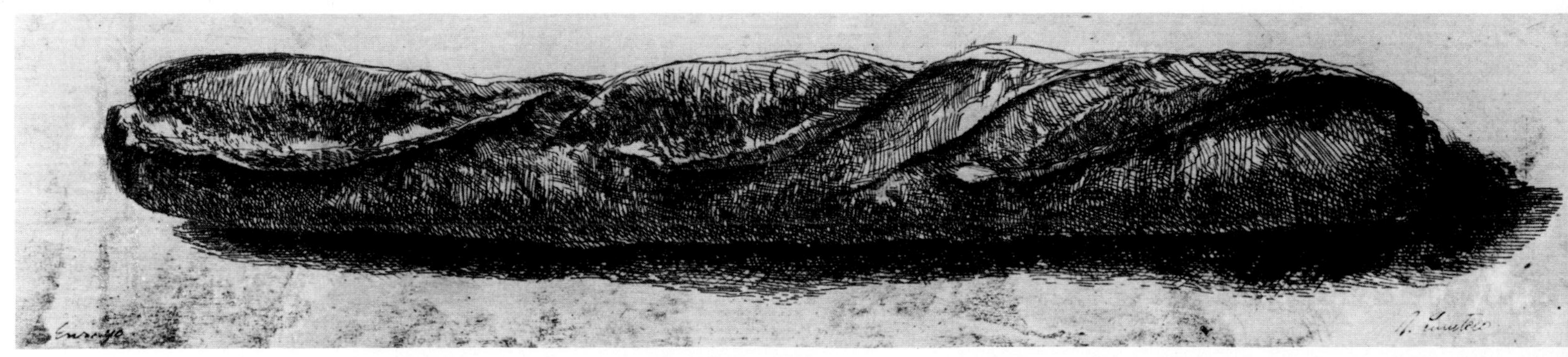

Daniel Quintero. *Quail with Grapes*. n.d. Dry point with retouching, 7⅞ × 9⅞". Private collection

QUAIL WITH GRAPES

4 quail
4 thin slices raw ham
½ cup dry white wine
½ cup grape juice
2 tablespoons butter
½ cup beef stock (or bouillon cube diluted)
4 small onions
Salt, pepper
1 small bunch of large green grapes, peeled

Clean the birds inside and outside. Cover each with a slice of ham. Put them in an earthenware dish and pour over them the white wine and grape juice. Dot with the butter. Cook in 400° for 10 minutes. Add the stock, onions, a very little salt, and pepper. Continue cooking another 15 minutes. Add the grapes and roast 10 minutes longer. Total cooking time: 35 minutes.

Serve in the roasting dish. Makes 2 servings

SOUPE BLANCHE

(White Gazpacho)

½ pound fresh almonds (to make 1⅓ cups finely chopped)
1 clove garlic, minced
2 tablespoons olive oil
White bread
Salt, pepper
1 or 2 bunches of green grapes

Crack the fresh almonds and heat them in a frying pan. Remove the skins and crush them in a mortar.

In a bowl combine the almonds, garlic, a little water, a trickle of olive oil, the bread, and salt and pepper and mix well. (This can also be done in the blender.)

Peel and seed the grapes and add them whole or sliced to the bread mixture. Stir energetically. Pour into cups with one ice cube per cup. The soup must be served chilled.
Makes 2 servings

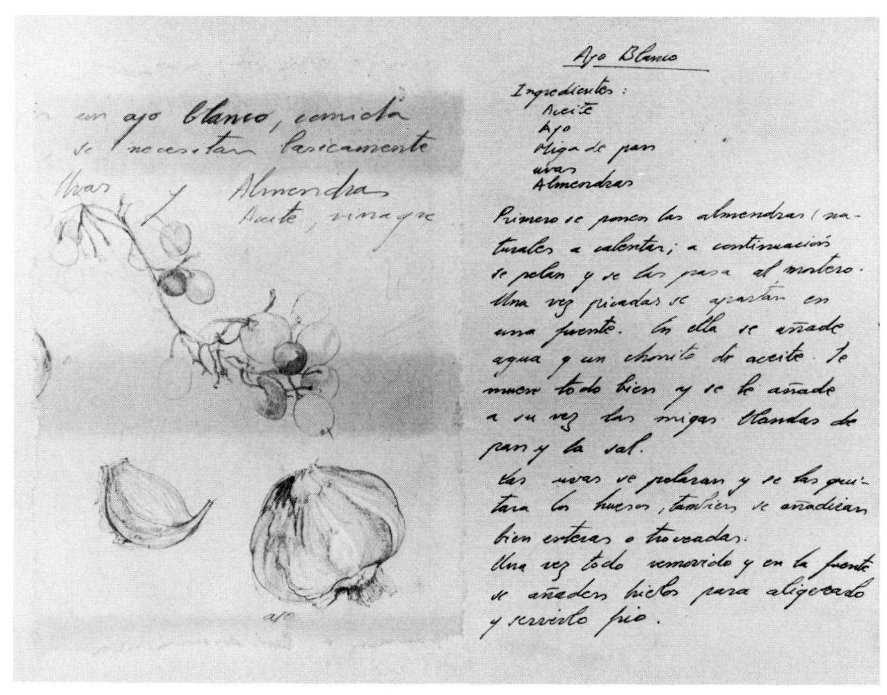

Daniel Quintero. *White Garlic Soup*. n.d. Pencil and colored pencils, 5⅛ × 6¾″.
Private collection

TROUT IN WHITE WINE

4 tablespoons butter
1 onion, chopped
1 carrot, sliced
1 stalk celery, chopped
Chopped parsley
Thyme
½ cup dry white wine
½ cup beef stock (or bouillon cube)
6 to 8 small potatoes
2 trout
Salt, pepper

Put 2 tablespoons butter and the onion, carrot, celery, parsley, and thyme in an earthenware dish. Brown them on the stove. When the mixture begins to take on color add the white wine, stock, and potatoes. Cook for 5 minutes. Salt and pepper the trout. Add them to the baking dish. Bake in the oven for 20 minutes, basting from time to time. Remove the fish and potatoes to a serving dish and keep warm. Add the remaining 2 tablespoons of butter to the sauce and simmer a few minutes. Pour the sauce over the trout and serve. Makes 2 servings

Daniel Quintero. *Trout*. n.d. Dry point, 7⅞ × 9⅞". Private collection

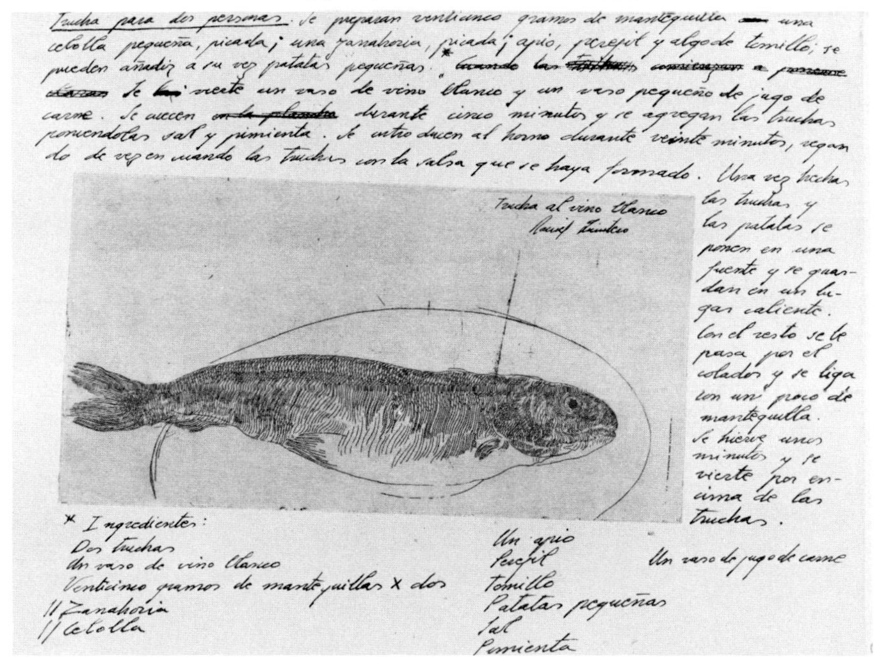

ANTONIO SAURA

Born 1930, Spain

Saura loves and appreciates elegant cooking. If he chose to hand on only this very simple recipe it was because the sandwich of fried squid is his personal equivalent of Proust's petite madeleine. *He is quick to admit that what he misses in Paris are certain smells of everyday Spanish cooking, odors profoundly intermingled with memories of his childhood and adolescence. Even now he has only to set foot in the Plaza Mayor in Madrid and all those seemingly lost fragments of his past come flooding—better, wafting—back.*

Fried squid on a plate with a squeeze of lemon is delicious. But in a sandwich the monster is, so to speak, tamed, and the contrast in taste between the soft white bread and the crisp squid is, Saura assures us, extraordinary. He is also fascinated by the sight of these mollusks stretching and twisting their tentacles in great pots of boiling oil. Saura says that in those many-armed bodies that seem to float in space there is something that reminds him of certain paintings by Kandinsky.

FRIED SQUID SANDWICH

½ pound or more of squid
Flour
Olive oil
Salt, pepper
1 roll

Clean the squid and slice into rings. Sprinkle with flour and fry in very hot oil. The squid are done when brown on both sides. Sprinkle with salt and pepper. Slice the roll in half and fill with the crisp squid. Makes 1 serving

"This is my favorite dish."

Antonio Saura. *Bocadillo de calamares fritos (Fried Squid Sandwich)*. 1979. India ink, $15\frac{3}{4} \times 22\frac{1}{2}$".
Private collection. © ADAGP 1987

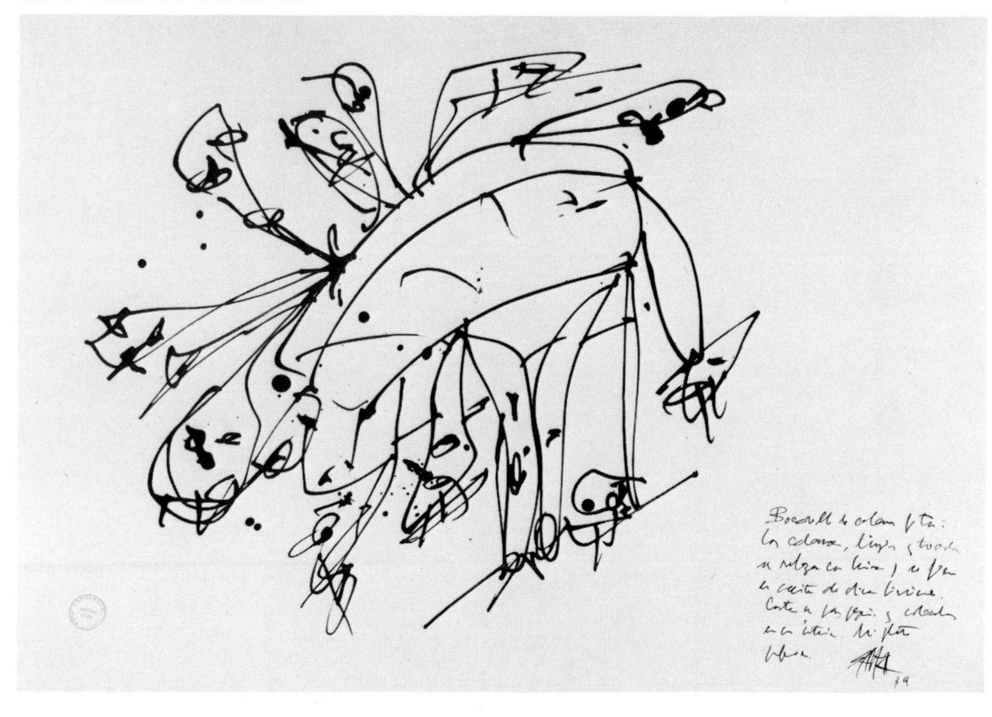

ANTONIO SEGUI

Born 1934, Argentina

You can invite Segui to come to your house in the country to prepare an asado *on your outdoor grill. He will accept with good grace and, to begin with, will get up at six in the morning and start digging a pit in the middle of your garden. Then he will make a slow fire and stand watch over it for hours, tending the embers so as not to stir up the flames. Once he has a good roasting fire smoldering, he displays his skill at manipulating the tongs as he turns the pieces of beef he has chosen with an artist's care—or an Argentine's, since that is saying almost the same thing when it comes to appreciating fine meat.*

His agility and dexterity are fascinating. His mustache seems to turn into expert antennae that can detect just the right cooking time. And then he serves one plate after another, accompanying each with a radiant smile (and watching out of the corner of his eye for every sign of your pleasure). His asado*? One more work of art!*

LEG OF MUTTON WITH FRUIT

2½ pound leg of mutton
4 cloves garlic
3 sprigs mint
Corn oil
Salt, pepper
2 pounds onions
2 pounds tomatoes
2 pounds sweet potatoes
1 pound chestnuts, canned
2 pounds russet apples

Make shallow cuts in the mutton and insert the garlic and mint. Set the joint in a roasting pan and coat with the oil. Add salt and pepper. Add the onions peeled and cut in half, the tomatoes peeled and quartered, and the sweet potatoes cut in large chunks. Roast in a 300° oven for 1 hour, basting every 15 minutes. Then add the chestnuts and the apples, peeled, cored, and cut in half, and continue roasting another 25 minutes. Makes 6 servings

CREOLE STEAKS

1 pound onions
3 tablespoons olive oil
2 pounds tomatoes
6 green peppers
6 large steaks, cut into thin slices
3 cloves garlic
Bay leaf
Salt, pepper
2 pounds potatoes
1 8-ounce can of peas

Peel and slice the onions in rounds. Melt them over low heat in 3 tablespoons of olive oil. Before they turn golden add the tomatoes cut in half, the peppers sliced in strips, the meat, garlic, bay leaf, salt, and pepper. Cover and let simmer over low heat. When just about cooked add the potatoes, sliced, and the green peas and cook another 20 minutes. Makes 6 servings

All drawings these pages:
Antonio Segui. Untitled. n.d. India ink, 9 × 11¾″.
Private Collection

ARGENTINE NOUGAT

1 pound butter
1 pound superfine sugar
1 pound bread crumbs
1 pound dried currants
1 pound roasted almonds
½ pound pine nuts
Zest of 10 lemons
½ pound lump sugar
Generous amount cinnamon (according to taste)

Blend the butter and superfine sugar in a heavy pot over low heat until they form a thick paste.

In a bowl mix the remaining ingredients. Add to the butter and sugar paste and stir constantly with a wooden spoon until the nougat becomes smooth and creamy and takes on a golden color. Cook over low heat another 10 to 15 minutes. Cool before serving.

YANNIS TSAROUCHIS

Born 1910, Greece

Yannis Tsarouchis is a child of Piraeus. He is a familiar figure in the inns at the port of Athens, a connoisseur of the local cuisine and folk dances, and one of the great painters of present-day Greece. He is also a philosopher who would have been able to hold his own in the agora, and for whom the Platonic dialectic no longer has any secrets. As a guest, he brings to the table a dazzling conversation. In short, he is a man of learning who does not think it beneath him to share what he knows either with soldiers or sailors.

In his paintings, Tsarouchis shows his fascination for these people. Sometimes we see them dancing in their taverns, other times soaring through space on angelic wings. In other paintings, wise young men are restored to a holier, purifying function: they are depicted haloed like saints in an icon, fixed in the hieratic dignity of disciples half-earnest, half-smiling at the word of the master, or bearing gifts of nature. With Tsarouchis the spiritual is never something distinct from the earthly. Four of his canvases, for instance, are devoted to germination and unfolding of the four seasons: gifts brought by a young man with a meditative mien. I sometimes find myself wondering if Tsarouchis will one day retire to Mount Athos and become a peasant-monk, nourishing himself with the products of his sheep, with tomatoes and peppers, becoming the Mediterranean sage he has been in some measure all his life.

STUFFED TOMATOES WITH BROWN RICE

2 ladles of brown rice
4 ladles of water
¼ cup olive oil
4 or 5 onions
1 clove garlic
1 handful pine nuts
2 handfuls currants or raisins
Salt
Basil
8 large tomatoes
Brown sugar
Potatoes, peeled and diced
Bread crumbs
Green peppers (optional)

Boil the brown rice in twice its volume of slightly salted water over low heat. When it is cooked turn off the heat and let it sit for 15 minutes uncovered. Melt 4 or 5 onions and 1 clove of garlic, all cut small, in olive oil. Add a handful of pine nuts and the currants. Add all this to the pot containing the rice and pour in a little olive oil along with some salt and minced basil.

Wash 8 large and perfect tomatoes and slice off the top to make a cap, without cutting all the way through. Salt the inside of the tomatoes and add a little crushed brown sugar. Carefully scoop out the pulp with a spoon; drain off the juice. Set the tomatoes in a baking dish and fill them with a diced potato. Combine the rice mixture with the tomato pulp and stuff each tomato. Again salt lightly and sprinkle the top with bread crumbs. You can also add a few green peppers among the tomatoes.

Bake in a 400° oven for 20 to 35 minutes. Best eaten cold. Makes 4 to 8 servings

OPPOSITE:
Yannis Tsarouchis. *Tomatoes and Peppers*. 1978. Watercolor, 18⅞ × 26⅝″

PAOLO VALLORZ

Born 1931, Italy

This portrait of a cèpe has a story behind it. When Paolo was a little boy in his village in the Dolomites, a neighbor got him to believe that he had taken shelter during a storm under a giant mushroom. True or not, this didn't discourage Paolo from developing a lifelong passion for mushrooms. He loves to hunt, paint, cook them au pif *as he puts it, and eat them. For many years, however, he subsisted on rice, which he scrupulously shared with his dog. His favorite meal is firmly in the peasant tradition: potato salad and good cheese. People who do not love cooking, he says, are a dry and cold lot.*

His greatest pleasure is to make a meal of six lemon tarts at La Coupole in Montparnasse, instead of the traditional entrée salad, and dessert. Alternately, he's distressed when a plate still half full is returned to the kitchen. Whence the drama every time he goes to a restaurant with his friend Riopelle. That master gourmand, who knows and frequents the best tables in France, hardly eats a thing. For Vallorz, it's useless to try to draw that.

APPLE "TORTEI"

4 apples (preferably russet)
¾ cup brown sugar
⅛ cup pine nuts
⅛ cup currants or raisins
Apple brandy (applejack, Calvados, grappa)
7 tablespoons butter
6 eggs

Peel and core the apples. Slice fine and combine with half of the brown sugar plus the pine nuts and currants. Steep in apple brandy for about 1 hour. Drain the apples (reserve the liquid) and sauté them with half the butter in a very hot skillet. Add the remaining brown sugar to caramelize the apples slightly. Beat the eggs as though for an omelet and add the reserved juice. Make an omelet; before the omelet is fully set fill it with the apple mixture. Fold, and set under the broiler to caramelize the sugar. Serve together with hot apple sauce made with apple brandy. Makes 4 servings

FIELD MUSHROOMS IN WINE VINEGAR

1½ pounds field mushrooms
2 tablespoons oil
2 bay leaves
1 stalk celery
1 clove garlic
Salt, pepper
¼ cup wine vinegar
Chives

Wash firm medium-size field mushrooms. Heat the oil in a skillet and add the whole mushrooms, bay leaves, the leaves from the celery stalk, a clove of unpeeled crushed garlic, and salt and pepper. When the mushrooms have released their moisture, cover with the wine vinegar. Raise the heat until the vinegar has evaporated. Remove the mushrooms from the pan, put the sauce through a strainer, and add finely chopped chives.

Excellent with roast game. Makes 4 servings

Paolo Vallorz. *Cèpe*. 1977. Oil on canvas, 7⅞ × 10⅝". Private collection

POLENTA WITH CÈPES

2 medium-size cèpes
2 tablespoons oil
2 shallots
1 clove garlic
1½ ounce prosciutto
3 tablespoons heavy cream
Salt, pepper
Parsley, chervil, chives

Clean the unwashed cèpes by scraping the dirt from the stalks and wiping the caps. Heat the oil in a sauté pan. Add 2 finely chopped shallots. When they have turned golden add the mushrooms cut in quite large pieces. Let them brown a little and give off their water. Separately chop the garlic and prosciutto (San Daniele, if possible). When the liquid from the mushrooms has evaporated, add the ham and garlic and let simmer for 1 minute. Add the cream and bring to a boil, then lower heat and stir until the sauce has thickened. Add salt and pepper. Transfer to a serving dish and sprinkle with finely chopped parsley, chervil, and chives. Serve with creamy polenta. Makes 2 servings

POLENTA

1 pound corn farina
Salt

In a copper pot, boil 2 cups salted water. Pour in the farina while stirring with a whisk until it is creamy. Cook over a low heat stirring with a wooden spoon, always in the same direction. When the mixture pulls from the sides of the saucepan, it is ready. Spoon the mixture into a square pan with high sides and brown in the oven.

It can be served in large slices, lightly toasted, or still slightly creamy.

MARIE-HÉLÈNE VIEIRA DA SILVA

Born 1908, Portugal

"Recipes? Why not?" replied Vieira da Silva. "But I do not think they will be very orthodox."
From "coq au vent" (rooster of the wind) to a compote of hearts made of roses which allows dew drops to fall on their petals, such things as the subtle flavors of a word, the perfume of an image, and the color of the sky make cooking and poetry rhyme for her.

COQ AU VENT

(Rooster of the Wind)

"The rooster on my church tower—deep roasted by the August sun, dried by the East wind, frozen in December by the Northeast winds—should be served cold, served on a weathervane, accompanied by dew from the Southwest."

Marie-Hélène Vieira da Silva. *The Grocer's.* 1969. Collage, 10⅝ × 8¼″.
Private collection. © ADAGP 1987

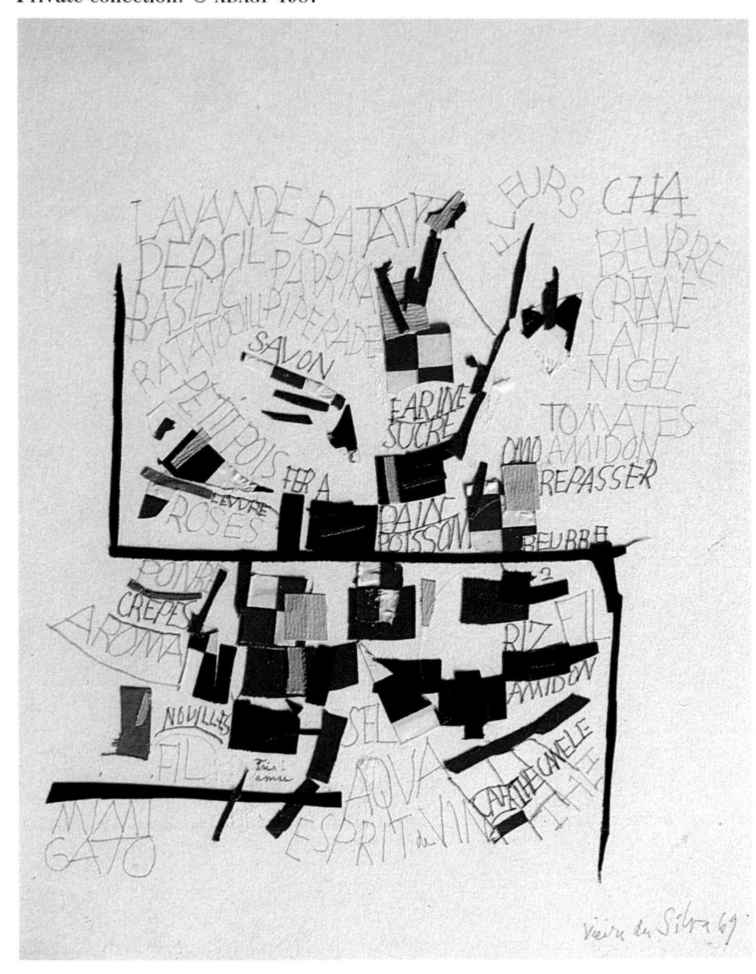

PAUL WIESENFELD

Born 1942, United States

An American who lives in Germany, Paul Wiesenfeld has a broad repertoire of recipes drawn from a variety of cuisines: Chinese, Mexican, Japanese, and Californian. Perhaps it's this culinary eclecticism that inspired him to evoke something eternally meridional in this quiet sun-drenched still life. Onion, lemon, grapes, an earthenware jug: a drawing that speaks of an entire civilization.

Paul Wiesenfeld. *Still life.* 1978. Pencil drawing, 11 7/16 × 16 1/2". Private collection

BARBECUED CHICKEN WITH SAUCE

2 chickens
1 tablespoon oil
Salt, pepper

Barbecue sauce
¼ cup olive or walnut oil
6 cloves garlic, chopped fine
1 small hot chili pepper, seeded, chopped fine
⅓ cup soy sauce
1 teaspoon powdered ginger or ½ teaspoon finely chopped ginger root
¼ cup sugar
2 tablespoons wine vinegar
4 tablespoons cayenne pepper
1 teaspoon cumin
1 teaspoon dry mustard
Salt, pepper
2 slices lemon
1 small can tomato paste
¼ teaspoon Tabasco
Pepper to taste

Cut the chickens in half lengthwise. Flatten the halves and rub them all over with oil and a little salt and pepper. Brush the pieces with the barbecue sauce and lay them on the grill (about 10 inches above the fire), flat side down. Roast 20 minutes, turn, and roast another 10 to 15 minutes. (If the pieces catch fire, douse the flame with a little water.) Baste with the sauce about every 6 minutes.

To prepare the sauce, heat the oil in a saucepan. Add the chopped garlic and chili pepper and cook a few minutes. Add the other ingredients, stirring with a wooden spoon over low heat, but do not let the sauce come to a boil. Simmer 7 to 8 minutes, stirring constantly. Make 4 servings

CHILI CON CARNE

2½ pounds chuck, ground or cubed
2 large onions
1 red pepper
1 green pepper
6 very ripe tomatoes
2 tablespoons tomato paste
¾ cup beef stock or 1 chicken bouillon cube, diluted
4 leaves fresh basil or 1 tablespoon dried
1 tablespoon cumin
1 red chili pepper
Salt and pepper to taste
1 8-ounce can of red beans (pinto or other)

Sauté the beef cut in small chunks or ground, which is more economical. Add the finely sliced onions and finely chopped green and red peppers. When the meat has browned slightly, add the chopped tomatoes along with the tomato paste, stock, basil, cumin, chili pepper, salt, and pepper. Simmer for 1 hour.

Add the red beans to the pot and cook over low heat another 10 minutes. Makes 6 to 8 servings

BORIS ZABOROV

Born 1937, U.S.S.R.

"One of the most moving memories of my life in Paris is that of the vernissage *of my first important show and the dinner afterward in a little restaurant on the Left Bank. Everyone at our table was particularly dear to me, but I was in a state of excitement and euphoria that called for something more. Nadine, with her wonderful charm, seeing me so moved and sensing what more I wanted called to me across the restaurant, 'I love you!' and I answered back with the same assurance.*

"It is the natural thing, after a declaration of love, to offer flowers. The next day I brought Nadine a 'bouquet' of cèpes. But that was no simple gastronomic gift. For us, in Byelorussia, it is a gift from the land. It represents both the colors and the subtle perfumes of our native soil. For me, it's a symbol.

"Being entirely unskilled in cooking I left it to my wife, an excellent cook, to write down the recipes for my three favorite dishes. Unfortunately, they can't bring back the very special taste and smell of these dishes, because the savor of food also depends on the soil that produces it."

Boris Zaborov. Untitled. 1984. Acrylic, 9 7/16 × 13". Private collection

BORSCHT

1 pound brisket or top ribs of beef
¼ green cabbage
1 carrot
½ red sweet pepper
Salt, pepper
2 potatoes
Thyme
Bay leaf
1 onion
Butter
2 or 3 tomatoes, chopped
1 beet, parboiled and peeled
1 or 2 cloves garlic
Dill, parsley, celery
Sour cream

Bring the meat to a boil in 1½ quarts of water. Skim from time to time. Cook for 2 hours, then add the chopped cabbage, sliced carrots, and red sweet pepper. Add salt and pepper and cook for 15 minutes. Add the potatoes, thyme, and bay leaf and cook another 15 minutes.

Meanwhile sweat the chopped onion in butter and add the tomatoes. Simmer a few minutes. Coarsely grate the beet.

Add all this to the soup pot along with 1 or 2 cloves of garlic and the dill, parsley, and celery. Let boil a few minutes.

Serve with sour cream and sprinkle with finely chopped herbs. Makes 4 to 5 servings

POTATO PANCAKES PEASANT-STYLE

6 or 7 large potatoes
1 teaspoon sugar
Salt, pepper
1 egg, lightly beaten
2 tablespoons flour
1 cup sunflower oil

Peel the potatoes and grate fine. Add the sugar to prevent discoloring. Add salt and pepper. Mix the lightly beaten egg with the flour and stir into the grated potatoes.

Heat the oil in a large skillet. Drop tablespoonfuls of the batter into the pan and fry them until they are brown and crusty on both sides. Serve hot.

"I like to eat these pancakes with the sautéed mushrooms in the following recipe."

MUSHROOMS SAUTÉED IN THE OLD STYLE

2 pounds small cèpes (preferably from Bordeaux)
1 stick butter
2 onions
Salt, pepper
½ pint cream

Use small cèpes, preferably freshly gathered.

Clean, wash, and dry the cèpes. Sauté in butter for 15 minutes, then remove from the heat and keep warm. Chop the onions, sprinkle with salt, and sweat over medium heat, stirring well until they are golden. Add the cream and pepper and bring to a boil. Pour the sauce over the mushrooms, stir, and serve.

Boris Zaborov. Untitled. 1984. Acrylic, 9⅞ × 9⅞″. Private collection

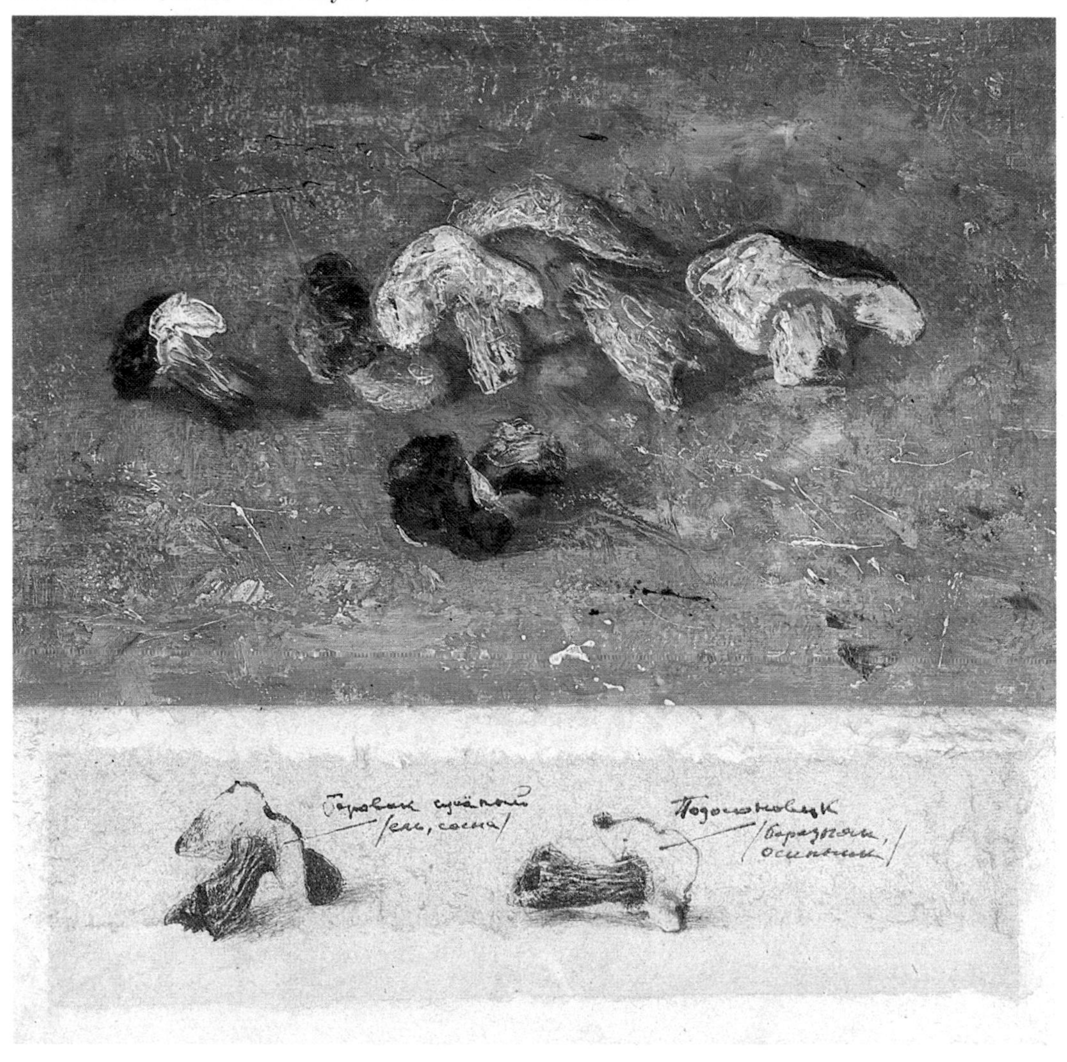

Christian Zeimert. *Eugène Boudin aux Pommes de Cézanne.* 1977. Pastel, 9 7/16 × 7⅞″

CHRISTIAN ZEIMERT

Born 1934, France

There is a good deal of humor in Christian Zeimert's paintings. In a series of works devoted to deflating the grandeur associated with the Great Painters, he amused himself by playing off their names—La Tour, Boucher, Millet (for little songbirds)—and took special delight when he could hit on some connection with painting: Szafran (as in paella), Bacon (as in eggs). Cubism gave him the idea for a recipe he called "Brouillon [implying both rough sketch and untidiness] of Magical Cubes." He leapt at the occasion to have me taste his Boudin with Apples à la Cézanne (which ties in the Impressionist painter Eugène Boudin and the familiar blood sausage that bears the same name). Christian is a timid man who never puts all his cards on the table. Except at table, *where he likes to eat a single dish until he is full, sometimes cucumbers in sour cream or, on fancier occasions, lobster à l'américaine. Generally, though, he'll insist that what he really prefers are simple country-style dishes that simmer on the stove for hours, like the* pot-au-feu *he used to cook on his studio stove in his bachelor years. Nowadays, though, he confines himself to cooking up his "delicious" canvases.*

BOUDIN WITH APPLES

8 apples
½ cup pork fat
4 serving portions blood sausage

Peel the apples, remove the seeds, and slice. In a skillet melt three-quarters of the pork fat till it is smoking hot. Then add the sliced apples. Lower heat. Do not stir; when they are well cooked let them form a kind of golden crêpe. (Do not add salt or pepper.) In another pan heat the remaining fat and fry the blood sausage 5 or 6 minutes on each side. The fat should sizzle a little.

Slide the apple crêpe onto a hot plate and cover with the blood sausages. Makes 4 servings

SOUPE AU CAILLOU

(Pebble Soup)

1 large pebble
1 pound salted pork shoulder butt
6 smoked sausages
¼ pound smoked bacon
1 small cabbage
1 pound combined carrots and turnips
1 onion studded with cloves
Bouquet garni
Pepper
2 pounds potatoes, peeled

Find a large pebble, clean it, dip it in boiling water, and lay it at the bottom of a large pot.

Soak the pork for 24 hours to remove any salt. Slice the pork. Combine in a pot with the smoked sausages, bacon, cabbage that has been blanched in boiling water, carrots and turnips, an onion stuck with cloves, the bouquet garni, and pepper. Cover with water and bring to a boil.

Gently boil for 2 hours over moderate heat. Do not add salt. Add the potatoes and cook another 30 minutes.

Dish up the vegetables and meat on a heated plate. If you like, serve the soup separately with fried croutons that have been rubbed with garlic. Makes 6 servings

CHERRY SOUP

2 to 3 slices country-style bread
1 stick plus 2 tablespoons butter
2 pounds black cherries, stemmed
¼ cup flour
½ cup sugar
2 tablespoons kirsch

Cut the bread into small cubes and fry them in half the butter. When they are golden remove them from the pan and set aside to cool. Pour off the butter and replace with fresh butter. When it has melted add the cherries and roll them in the flour. Moisten with just enough water to cover, then sprinkle on the sugar. Cook for 30 minutes. Five minutes before the end of cooking add 2 tablespoons of kirsch. When the cherries are well cooked and the syrup smoothly blended, lay the croutons in a dish and cover with the cherries and syrup. Serve hot. Makes 4 servings

BRAINS EN BROCHETTE, BOURGEOIS-STYLE

2 calf's brains, previously soaked, trimmed, and blanched
¼ pound veal udder (or ¼ pound bacon)
1 small can sliced truffles
3 tablespoons oil
Parsley
Salt, pepper
3 tablespoons butter
¼ cup flour

Cut the brains into large cubes and likewise the udder, which has been previously cooked and cooled. Marinate in a little oil with the truffles, chopped parsley, salt, and pepper. Thread on skewers alternating the brains, udder (or bacon), and truffles. Brush each skewer with a little oil and butter. Roll the skewers in flour and grill over a hot fire. Makes 4 servings

PIKE AU BEURRE BLANC

For the court bouillon
1 carrot
2 onions
Parsley
Salt, pepper

Beurre blanc
10 shallots
1 pint dry white wine
7 tablespoons butter
Salt, pepper

1 medium-size pike (about 4 pounds)

Prepare the court bouillon in advance. Boil 1 carrot, 2 onions, parsley, salt, and pepper in a quart of water for 25 minutes. Let cool.

Clean the fish well, inside and out (discard any eggs). Put it in the cooled court bouillon and bring to a boil. Then lower the heat and cook gently for about 20 minutes.

For the beurre blanc: peel and chop the shallots and cook them in the dry white wine about 25 minutes until they are easily crushed. Transfer to a bain-marie (do not have the water too hot). Add the butter in small pieces, all the time stirring to make a smooth sauce, then beat energetically with a whisk. Serve alongside the fish in a warm sauce bowl.

NADINE IN THE KITCHEN

This cookbook wouldn't have the same savor if, after having explored the culinary secrets of her painter friends, Nadine Haim didn't reveal her own expertise in the kitchen. Hers, in fact, is a true talent. Whatever she prepares is a treat for the eyes, the taste buds, and the imagination. One might think of her as "Everybody's Mother," someone who greets you with a smile and a good meal. Some friends have nicknamed her "Tante Nadine," the proverbial aunt and loving mother. Regardless of the culture or the time, women have excelled at cooking. Certainly there are men who cook well, but it may be that many of them—including the painter-cooks who figure in these pages—learned by watching their mothers in the kitchen.

Nadine has an adventurous spirit—wherever she happens to be she's eager to taste new foods and collect recipes (and corkscrews on the side), haunt the local markets, and bring home exotic ingredients, spices, herbs with mysterious perfumes. She is not one to settle for routine in the kitchen. She prefers to invent, and experiment, to concoct menus that transport one to different cultures. Store-bought or prepared foods have no place in her kitchen.

Another thing about Nadine is that however complicated her work is in the kitchen, you would never guess it from the look of the place. The kitchen is no less presentable at dinnertime than her pleasurable table setting—they both convey the same elegance, the same originality. All signs of effort have vanished, there is no trace of the hours spent preparing a dinner perfect in every detail. Nadine makes her guests feel she is one of them, utterly relaxed, neither fussing nor fatigued. And that is a special gift, a sure sign of friendship. But it is also, have no doubt, an art. Nadine's other art.

SOPHIE LANNES

BOUILLON COCKTAIL WITH VODKA

1 jigger vodka
2 or 3 drops Tabasco sauce
5 or 6 drops Worcestershire sauce
½ cup bouillon (or pot-au-feu stock)

In a whiskey glass combine 1 jigger of vodka with the Tabasco and Worcestershire. Add very hot bouillon and stir.

Can be drunk cold as well.

TOMATOES WITH ANCHOVY PURÉE

6 ripe tomatoes
6 anchovy fillets
1 tablespoon *each:* parsley, chervil, chives
1 teaspoon oregano
Juice of 1 lemon
Olive oil
Pepper

Wash the tomatoes and quarter them. Mix the anchovies with the chopped parsley, chervil, chives, and oregano. Add the lemon juice, olive oil, and pepper, and stir into a thick sauce. Pour the sauce over the tomato quarters in a salad bowl and chill for 1 hour before serving. Makes 6 servings

STUFFED ORANGES

(an hors d'oeuvre)

6 oranges
1 can sardines in oil
Yolks of 2 hard-boiled eggs
2 tablespoons capers
2 teaspoons mustard
2 tablespoons chopped chervil
6 black or green olives, for garnish

Cut off one end of each orange. Remove the pulp without breaking the peel. Reserve the juice of 1 orange.

Drain the sardines and mash them with a fork. Add the egg yolks, capers, mustard, chervil, and the orange juice. Mix well.

Stuff the oranges with this preparation and decorate each with an olive. Makes 6 servings

FRESH SOUP

3 large ripe avocados
About 7 cups chicken consommé
Cayenne pepper, salt
1 cup or more cream

Peel the avocados and discard the seed. Mash the flesh in the mixer. Warm the consommé (or diluted cubes) slightly and stir the puréed avocado into it. Season, add the cream, and blend in the mixer again.

Chill 3 to 4 hours before serving. Makes 6 servings

EGGPLANT CAVIAR

6 large eggplants
1 onion
Juice of 1½ lemons
¼ cup oil
Salt, pepper

Preheat the oven to 500°. Wash the eggplants and cut off the stems. Dry them and lay them directly on the grate in the oven (it is best to place a sheet of aluminum foil underneath them). Roast for 45 minutes, turning frequently to roast on all sides. Remove from the oven, cut them in half, and scrape the flesh into a bowl. Peel the onion and chop coarsely. Put the eggplant, lemon juice, onion, oil, and salt and pepper into the mixer and give a few spins to obtain a delicate purée. Chill for 2 hours before serving. Will keep 2 days. Makes 6 servings

PÂTÉ DE FOIES DE VOLAILLE

(Chicken Liver Pâté)

For 1 terrine, about 12 inches in diameter
4 tablespoons goose fat
¾ pound onions
1¼ pounds chicken livers
1 tablespoon thyme
Salt, pepper
1 truffle

Melt the goose fat in a skillet. Add the peeled and thinly sliced onions and cook over low heat. Remove when the onions are soft. Add the coarsely chopped livers, thyme, and salt and pepper. Cook 5 to 6 minutes. Blend the onions and livers in a mixer. Add the truffle cut into small pieces and transfer the pâté to an earthenware terrine. Chill for 5 to 6 hours.

COUSCOUS SALAD

1 pound couscous semolina
Juice of 6 lemons
4 small onions
1 cucumber
6 medium-size tomatoes

Dressing
1¼ cups olive oil
½ cup fresh mint leaves
3 tablespoons minced parsley
Salt, pepper

Steam the couscous grains for 6 minutes. Put them in a large salad bowl, pour lemon juice over them, and mix well until moist.

Cut the onions and cucumbers into thin slices and chop the tomatoes. Mix with the couscous and let sit for 3 hours.

To prepare the dressing, combine the oil, mint, parsley, and salt and pepper. Thirty minutes before serving, add the dressing to the salad and chill in the refrigerator. Makes 6 servings

CUCUMBERS WITH MINT

2 cucumbers
1 plain yogurt
3 drops Tabasco sauce
5 sprigs fresh mint
Salt, pepper

Peel the cucumbers and slice thin. Crisp them in salted water. Drain and pat dry with a cloth. Blend the yogurt, Tabasco, mint, and pepper and pour over the cucumbers in a salad bowl.

Chill for 1 hour before serving. Makes 4 servings

APPLE COMPOTE WITH ORANGE ZEST

2 pounds apples
¾ cup superfine sugar
Orange zest
1 cinnamon stick

Peel, core, and quarter the apples and put them in water. Melt the sugar in ¾ cup of water over low heat together with the orange zest and cinnamon stick. When it has become syrupy, add the quartered apples and cook for 15 to 20 minutes. Turn into a compote bowl (together with the syrup), let cook, then chill in the refrigerator. Before serving remove the cinnamon. Makes 4 servings

PRUNES IN RED WINE

1 pound dried prunes
1½ cups red wine (Burgundy)
½ cup superfine sugar
1 vanilla bean
Peel of 2 oranges
A few orange slices, for garnish

Soak the prunes for 1 hour in cold water. Drain. Cover with wine in a saucepan and add the sugar, vanilla bean, and orange peel. Bring to a boil, then lower heat and cook for 30 minutes. Remove from heat. When the prunes have cooled, transfer them to a compote dish and decorate with orange slices. Makes 4 servings

CORN SOUFFLÉ

1 12-ounce can corn kernels
3 tablespoons butter
½ cup heavy cream
3 whole eggs, separated plus 1 egg white
Salt, pepper

Mash the corn and grind it in a mixer or blender. Melt the butter in a saucepan, add the corn, and cook for a few minutes over low heat, stirring with a wooden spoon. Add the cream little by little to obtain a smooth purée. Remove from the heat and add 3 egg yolks, salt, and pepper and mix well. Beat 4 egg whites until very firm and fold them into the purée. Spoon into a buttered soufflé dish and bake in a 400° oven for 20 minutes; do not open the door. Makes 4 servings

OMELET FANNY

2 pounds leeks
Salty cheese
Goat cheese
¼ pound Parmesan cheese
10 eggs
Pepper
2 tablespoons oil
Butter

Cook the leeks in unsalted water the night before. Drain them, press out the water, wrap the leeks in a towel, and keep them in the refrigerator overnight. The next day, chop the leeks. Crumble the cheeses into a bowl. Beat the eggs, add to the cheese, and beat the mixture (best in an electric blender) to make a velvety purée. Add the chopped leeks. Add pepper but *no* salt. Pour the preparation into an oiled or buttered baking dish and top with a dozen small slices of butter. Bake in a 350° oven for 25 minutes. To check when the omelet has cooked through, prick it with the point of a knife: if it comes out dry the omelet is ready. Serve cooked or lukewarm, but not hot. Makes 6 servings

OMELET WITH WALNUTS AND ROQUEFORT

12 eggs
¼ pound Roquefort
10 to 12 walnuts, chopped
2 tablespoons apple brandy (applejack, Calvados)
Salt, pepper
5 tablespoons butter or lard

Beat the eggs in a large bowl and mix in the crumbled Roquefort and chopped walnuts. Add the apple brandy (Calvados if you have it), salt, and pepper and beat energetically.

Melt the butter or lard in a large omelet pan and pour in the eggs. Once the omelet has set, fold and serve. Makes 6 servings

PASTA SHELLS WITH WALNUTS AND MINT

1½ pounds small pasta shells
¾ cup shelled walnuts
1 tablespoon fresh mint
¾ cup bouillon (or diluted beef cube)
1½ cups oil
Salt, pepper

Boil the pasta shells for 20 minutes in abundant salted water. Drain well and keep warm. While the pasta is cooking, crush the walnuts with a rolling pin or bottle, chop the mint, and warm the bouillon.

Heat oil in a fireproof serving dish and add the pasta. Stir in the walnuts, mint, and salt and pepper. Pour in the bouillon and stir with a wooden spatula. Equally delicious cold. Makes 6 servings

FETTUCCINI WITH SMOKED SALMON

½ pound freshly made fettuccini
¼ pound smoked salmon
3 tablespoons olive oil
½ cup heavy cream
Salt, pepper

Cook the fettuccini in abundant salted water. Meanwhile, use a scissors to cut the salmon into small rectangles. When the pasta is ready, drain it and rinse rapidly with cold water. Heat the oil in a large saucepan, add the pasta, and swirl about to coat the pasta. Add the salmon and cream, stirring with a wooden spoon. Serve in a warm dish. Makes 4 servings

TUNA FISH "SHALOM"

1 fresh tuna fish
Juice of 2 or 3 lemons
Salt
1 quart olive oil
1 head garlic
Thyme
Bay leaf
Oregano
1 cup vinegar
1 pinch red pepper flakes

When you come back from catching a tuna fish, before preparing it for cooking you must drain the blood, and you can do this right on the boat by cutting a slit behind the gills and squeezing the tail toward the head to force out the blood.

To prepare, cut the fish in slices about 1½-inch thick. Sprinkle with lemon juice and salt, and leave overnight in the refrigerator.

The next day, pat the slices dry with a paper towel. Fry the tuna very quickly in an earthenware pot containing 1 quart of the hot oil. To the same oil add the whole head of garlic, which should be unpeeled but crushed slightly, plus the thyme, bay leaf, oregano, and vinegar. Sizzle for 5 minutes, then return the tuna to the oil for further frying, adding also the red pepper. Remove from the oil, drain, and let cool.

This tuna "Shalom" can be preserved in a jar with oil. The taste is similar to that of a very fine canned tuna. It is excellent accompanied by a tomato salad.

TROUT WITH HERBS

6 trout
Juice of 3 lemons
Rosemary
Sage
Savory
Thyme
Bay leaf
1½ sticks butter, at room temperature
1 shallot
Salt, pepper

Scale and clean the trout and marinate them for 15 minutes on each side in the lemon juice, herbs, butter, shallot, salt, and pepper. Bake them in a 375° oven, still in the marinade, 10 minutes on each side, basting from time to time. Makes 6 servings

WHITEFISH FILLETS WITH ALMONDS

½ pound almonds, peeled
3 tablespoons butter
1½ pounds whitefish fillets
1 cup dry white wine
Juice of 1 lemon
Salt, pepper

Toast the almonds in the butter and add the white wine. In a separate pan fry the fish fillets. When done add the lemon juice and salt and pepper. Pour the almonds and wine over the fish and serve. Makes 4 servings

BEIGNETS D'ACRA

¼ pound salt cod
1¾ cups flour
1 cup milk
2 eggs
1 clove garlic
1 shallot
1 onion
Pepper
Red chili pepper
Oil

Soak the cod for 5 or 6 hours to remove salt. Drain.

Combine the flour, milk, and eggs in a bowl to make a batter. Crush the fish very fine in a mortar and boil it in water for 10 minutes with the garlic, shallot, onion, and black pepper. Drain and stir into the batter. Add red pepper to taste.

Heat oil in a deep fryer. When hot, add spoonfuls of the batter, taking care that the beignets remain separate in the oil. They are done when they swell and become golden. Dry on paper towels before serving. Makes 4 servings

FROG LEGS WITH CALVADOS

8 pairs of frog legs
1 tablespoon flour
5 tablespoons butter
6 shallots, chopped
Parsley, minced
1 clove garlic, chopped
Salt, pepper
1½ cups milk
1 egg yolk
¼ pound Gruyere, grated
Bread crumbs
Calvados

Dust the frog legs with flour, fry them in butter for 4 minutes or until well browned, add the chopped shallots, parsley, garlic, salt, and pepper.

Make a béchamel sauce with butter, flour, and the 1½ cups of milk. Add the egg yolk, grated cheese, and salt and pepper, and cook another minute. Arrange the frog legs in a buttered baking dish and pour the sauce over them. Sprinkle with bread crumbs. Bake in a 400° oven for 5 minutes. Just before serving, pour Calvados over the dish and ignite it.

BOULETTES BINI

(Minorcan Fish Balls)

1 onion, chopped
1 clove garlic
1 pimiento
1 bunch parsley
Salt, pepper
2 pounds fish fillets, such as flounder
½ pound sliced bread
Milk
1 cup peanut oil

For the sauce
2 onions
3 carrots
3 turnips
½ medium-size cabbage
2 potatoes
4 tablespoons oil
1 cup tomato paste
Thyme
Bay leaf
Salt, pepper

Bini is a Minorcan word for "home," thus "homemade" boulettes.

In a wooden mortar mash the onion, garlic, pimiento, and chopped parsley; then mix with a drop of oil, salt, and pepper. Add the raw fish. Combine to make a well-blended paste. Soak the bread in a very little milk, squeeze any excess, and mix with the fish. With slightly oiled hands shape the mixture into small balls. Brown the balls in hot oil in a frying pan. Remove from the pan and keep warm.

Peel and chop the onions. Slice the vegetables. Heat the oil in a large pan and brown the onions. Add the tomato paste diluted with a little water. Return the fish balls to the pan and add some more water. When the liquid is simmering, add all the sliced vegetables, thyme, bay leaf, and salt and pepper, and cook over low heat for 15 minutes.

RED SNAPPER WITH FENNEL

2 red snapper (about 1½ pounds)
Oil
2 sticks plus 5 tablespoons butter
About ¼ pound fennel, blanched and chopped
Juice of ½ lemon
Salt, pepper

Scale, clean, rinse, and dry the snapper. Put a trickle of oil on each and lay them on or under a preheated grill. Allow 10 minutes for each side. Remove, and season with salt and pepper.

For the sauce: melt the butter over low heat, add the chopped fennel, lemon juice, salt and pepper, and stir to mix. Serve with the fish. Makes 6 servings

EELS "BINIBÉCOISES"

1½ pounds eel, skinned and cleaned
12 small onions
9 tablespoons butter
Salt, pepper
1 pint dry white wine
1 clove garlic, chopped
2 tablespoons flour
Lemon slices, for garnish

Cut the eel into 3-inch pieces. Brown the onions in 7 tablespoons of the butter in a frying pan. Add the eel, salt, pepper, wine, and chopped garlic and cook over moderate heat for 25 minutes. Remove from the heat. Drain the sauce into another saucepan and blend in the remaining 2 tablespoons butter. Stir in the flour plus a little wine. Cook over low heat a few minutes and pour over the eel. Decorate the serving platter with lemon slices.

LOBSTER SOUFFLÉ

1 can lobster bisque
½ cup milk
6 eggs, separated
½ cup grated Gruyère
3 tablespoons butter

Warm the bisque in a bain-marie. Transfer it to another pot with the milk. Stir over low heat with a wooden spoon; remove from the heat. Blend in the egg yolks one by one, and stir in the grated cheese. Beat the egg whites until firm and gently fold them into the lobster base. Butter a soufflé mold, pour in the mixture, and bake in a 400° oven for about 30 minutes until firm. Makes 6 servings

LANGOUSTES FLAMBÉES IN WHISKEY

(Crayfish Flambé)

4 crayfish
Court bouillon
Oil
Whiskey

For the sauce
2 sticks butter
Juice of 2 lemons
Parsley
Salt, pepper

Count on one crayfish per person. Cook for 15 minutes in a court bouillon. Remove and set aside to cool. Cut each crayfish in half lengthwise with a scissors, beginning with the tail. Prepare a wood fire. When the wood is well and truly glowing, grill the crayfish first on the back (10 minutes), then pour a trickle of oil over them and add salt and pepper. Turn and grill another 10 minutes.

For the sauce: melt the butter in a saucepan. Add the lemon juice and a handful of finely chopped parsley. Do not let the sauce come to a boil, but keep hot.

When ready to serve, flambé the crayfish with a good dose of whiskey. Serve on an oblong platter; pass sauce separately.

White rice served with this goes beautifully with the lemon sauce. Makes 4 servings

CRAYFISH WITH CAYENNE PEPPER

2½ pounds crayfish
Oil for deep frying
8 ripe red tomatoes (or 1 small can tomato paste)
2 tablespoons oil
1 sugar cube
Salt
Cayenne pepper
Savory
1 cup dry white wine
4 tablespoons cream

Wash the crayfish and with the point of a knife remove the intestine (the small black fillet in the tail). Sauté the crayfish in hot oil; remove when they take on color.

In a large copper frying pan, combine the peeled and seeded tomatoes with a little oil and sugar, salt, cayenne pepper, and savory. Bring to a boil. Cover and let simmer for 15 to 20 minutes. Add the white wine. Add the crayfish to the sauce and simmer for another 10 to 15 minutes. Reduce heat and stir in the cream. Check the seasoning, which should be fiery and peppery. Serve hot.

TURKEY CUTLETS WITH CURRY

4 turkey cutlets
Ginger
3 onions
1 apple
¼ cup oil
1½ tablespoons curry powder
½ cup grated coconut
2 cups hot water
Salt, pepper
1 pinch paprika
2 tablespoons cream

Sprinkle the turkey with ginger. Peel the onions and chop fine. Grate the apple.

Sauté the turkey slices in hot oil with the onions until they are golden on both sides. Add the curry powder, grated coconut, and the apple. Stir over high heat for a few minutes. Pour in the hot water and add salt, pepper, and a pinch of paprika. Bring to a simmer, add the cream and simmer a while longer. Serve with boiled rice. Makes 4 servings

POULET ELDA

One 1-2¼ pound chicken
Juice of 1 lemon
1 clove garlic, peeled
Salt, pepper
1 cup flour
1 cup milk
2 tablespoons oil
2 tablespoons butter

Cut the chicken into pieces and marinate for 6 to 8 hours in the refrigerator with the lemon juice, garlic, salt, and pepper.

Coat the chicken with some of the flour. Stir the milk into the lemon marinade and continue marinating the chicken for 1 hour. Flour the pieces once again and let them sit for 30 minutes. Fry the chicken in the oil and butter for 20 to 25 minutes.

Plain rice goes well with this dish.

ROAST CHICKEN

1 young chicken
1 lemon
1 chicken bouillon cube
3 tablespoons butter
Salt, pepper

Select a nicely plump chicken. Clean it inside and out. Stuff it with a whole lemon (washed) and the bouillon cube. Sew up and roast the chicken for 30 minutes. Then add ½ cup of water and scrape up any bits on the bottom of the pan. Roast another 30 minutes, basting frequently. Chop the giblets fine and cook them in a small pot with the butter and salt and pepper to make a sauce to accompany the chicken.

CHICKEN VELL

(a Minorcan dish)

1 chicken
Oil
2 cloves of garlic
Juice of 2 lemons
Salt, pepper

Cut the chicken into pieces, breaking the joints of the wings and legs. Heat the oil in a casserole. When hot, place the chicken in the pot along with the unpeeled but lightly crushed garlic cloves. When the pieces are golden brown, remove them from the heat and add the lemon juice. Cook briefly. Return the chicken and cook for 15 to 20 minutes. Season when ready to serve. Makes 4 servings

CHICKEN KEBOBS WITH RED PEPPER

1 large chicken
Juice of 4 lemons
Rosemary
Red pepper
Salt

Remove the skin and cut the chicken into pieces. Thread the skewers with the chicken and marinate for 20 minutes in the lemon juice and rosemary. Remove and dry with paper towels.

Sprinkle with salt and red pepper. Grill the kebobs over a hot wood or charcoal fire, turning frequently. Makes 8 servings

STUFFED BREAST OF LAMB

3-pound lamb breast, boned
1 cup raisins
⅛ cup Armagnac
¼ pound country-style ham
⅔ pound sausage meat
1 cup bread crumbs
½ cup milk
1 clove garlic
Parsley
2 eggs, beaten
Salt, pepper

Have the butcher prepare the lamb breast for stuffing. Soak the raisins in Armagnac. When they are plump, drain (reserve liquid), and mix them with the chopped ham, sausage meat, bread crumbs soaked in milk, crushed garlic, a handful of chopped parsley, the beaten eggs, and salt and pepper. Stuff the breast, and sew the edges together so the stuffing will not fall out during roasting. Rub with lard and roast for 1 hour and 20 minutes in a 350° oven, basting frequently.

Before serving, make a glaze of the drippings in the roasting pan with the brandy in which the raisins were soaked. Serve the sauce with the lamb. Makes 6 servings

LAMB WITH CUMIN

3 pounds lamb shoulder
1¼ sticks butter
3 tablespoons cumin
Mint jelly
Currant jelly

Heat the oven to high. Put the lamb in a pyrex or earthenware dish. Season with salt and pepper. Cover it entirely with bits of butter so that one can barely see the meat. Dust both sides liberally with the cumin.

Roast for 20 minutes at a high temperature, then reduce the heat and cook for another 40 minutes. Total cooking time should be about 1 hour. Do not baste as the skin should be crisp.

Serve the meat in thin slices accompanied by the mint jelly and currant jelly. Makes 6 servings

ROAST LOIN OF PORK WITH PINEAPPLE

Pork tenderloin (allow about ½ pound per person)
30 cloves
1 large can pineapple slices
3 tablespoons butter
Pepper, very little salt

Stud the loin with 20 or so cloves. Melt the butter in a roasting pan and brown the meat on all sides. Cut half the pineapple slices in two, setting aside the juice. Stud them with the remaining cloves and add to the pan, turning them so as to coat with the butter. Pour the pineapple juice over the meat. Roast in a 325° oven in the covered pan, allowing 30 minutes per pound.

Decorate the serving platter with wedges of fresh pineapple. Slice the roast and arrange the slices in the middle of the dish with some of the sauce and the cooked pineapple. Serve the remaining sauce on the side.

KIDNEYS WITH MUSTARD

12 lamb kidneys
5 tablespoons butter
2 tablespoons apple brandy (Calvados)
3 tablespoons sharp mustard
1½ cups heavy cream
Salt, white pepper

Slice the kidneys in two but without separating the halves. Sear rapidly on both sides in half the butter.

Melt the remaining butter in a heatproof casserole, add the kidneys, and cook gently for 2 to 3 minutes. Pour in the apple brandy and light the liqueur. Add the mustard, cream, salt, and pepper and swirl the kidneys around until coated. Serve immediately before they toughen. Makes 6 servings

BRAISED OXTAIL WITH CARROTS

2 pounds oxtail, cut into 2-inch pieces
3 tablespoons oil
2 onions, sliced
2¼ cups red wine
1 cup water
Salt, pepper
2 pounds carrots, trimmed
Thyme
Bay leaf
Tarragon

Brown the oxtail in the oil in a good-sized casserole. Add the sliced onions and cook for a few minutes, then add the wine and water. Season with salt and pepper and cook over low heat for 3 hours with the carrots, thyme, bay leaf, and tarragon. Before serving, degrease and serve the oxtail with the sauce.

QUAIL WITH GINGER

8 quail
½ pound smoked bacon
2½ sticks butter
Salt, pepper
1 tablespoon powdered ginger
1 cup dry white wine

Clean the quail. Melt the butter in a large casserole and brown the bacon which has been cut into cubes. Place the quail in the dish and brown them quickly at a high temperature for 8 to 10 minutes, turning often, Add salt, pepper, and ginger. Pour in the white wine. Cover and cook at a low temperature for 20 minutes.

Heat the platter. Arrange the birds with some of the sauce on top and the rest in a sauce boat. Makes 4 servings

PHEASANT WITH VINE LEAVES

1 good-sized pheasant
1 slice bacon
2 vine leaves
Salt, pepper
1¼ sticks butter, melted

Preheat the oven to 400°. Bard the pheasant and cover the bird with the leaves. Season the bird. Place in a roasting pan with the melted butter. Place in the oven to brown on all sides, basting with the juices. After 25 minutes, remove the bacon and vine leaves. Cook for another 10 minutes (the more one bastes, the juicier the pheasant will be). Total cooking time should be around 30-35 minutes. The dish can be served with a purée of cooking apples and blueberry jam. Makes 4 servings

ROAST SQUABS WITH WALNUTS

Stuffing
⅓ cup raisins
6 tablespoons cognac
2 to 3 slices day-old bread
¼ cup milk
1½ ounces shelled walnuts
Livers and hearts of the squabs
1 egg, beaten
Salt, pepper

4 squabs
4 strips bacon
6 tablespoons butter
2 carrots
1½ onions
Bouquet garni
Salt, pepper
4 slices white bread
10 walnuts, for garnish

To make the stuffing, soak the raisins in cognac for 2 hours and soak the bread in the milk. Chop the shelled walnuts with the squab livers and hearts and mix with the egg. Squeeze the bread and drain the raisins. Add to the stuffing with some salt and pepper.

Stuff the birds, season with salt and pepper, crisscross the bacon strips around the birds, and truss. Melt 3 tablespoons of the butter in a roasting pan and brown the birds on all sides. Add the carrots and onions cut into pieces and the bouquet garni. Bake in a 350° oven, uncovered, for 10 minutes, then cover and bake for 1 hour.

Cut the bread slices to make triangles and brown them in the remaining butter in a sauté pan.

Serve the squab on a platter garnished with the croutons and walnut halves. Makes 4 servings

COCONUT SOUFFLÉ

7 egg yolks
6 tablespoons sugar
1 cup grated coconut
1½ tablespoons whiskey
2 teaspoons Cointreau
6 egg whites
Butter
Powdered sugar

Heat the oven to maximum. Beat the egg yolks, add 6 tablespoons of sugar, and whip until the mixture is smooth and thick. Heat this mixture in a double boiler and stir with a wooden spoon until the sauce has thickened. Add the coconut, whiskey, and Cointreau. Pour the mixture into a large bowl and chill over ice, stirring again.

Beat the egg whites and fold them carefully into the now cooled mixture. Butter the bottom and sides of a straight-sided 6-cup soufflé dish and dust lightly with powdered sugar. Pour the mixture into the mold, but do not fill it completely. Level the surface and make a spiral with a wooden spoon. Place in the preheated hot oven. After 5 minutes reduce the heat to 350° and bake another 15 to 25 minutes. Check to see that the soufflé has puffed and turned golden. Before serving, dust with powdered sugar.

FRUIT SALAD WITH ALMONDS

2 apples
Juice of ½ lemon
2 pears
3 oranges
1 banana
½ pound raspberries
½ cup sugar
½ pound almonds, shelled and peeled

Peel and quarter the apples and sprinkle them with lemon juice to prevent discoloring. This also gives them a nice flavor. Peel the pears and cut them into quarter-inch slices. Remove the white pith from the oranges and slice them. Peel the banana and slice into thin rounds. Combine the fruit in a compote dish along with the raspberries. Sprinkle with ¼ cup of the sugar.

In a small saucepan make a syrup of the remaining ¼ cup sugar and ¼ cup of water. When the syrup is thick, stir in the almonds. When they have become golden, remove the syrup from the heat and pour it over the fruit. Chill before serving. Makes 5 to 6 servings

GÂTEAU TOMASA

7 tablespoons soft butter
3 eggs, separated
3 tablespoons sugar
40 petits-beurre or other plain butter cookie
Nescafé
Grated chocolate
¼ cup (or more) ground almonds

Blend the butter, egg yolks, and sugar with a fork. Beat the egg whites and fold them into the egg mixture.

In a rectangular dish about 2 inches deep make a layer of the petits-beurre, previously soaked in very strong Nescafé, setting them face down. Spread with the creamy mixture and repeat layering. Sprinkle the top layer with grated chocolate and ground almonds.

Chill for 4 hours in the refrigerator. Even better prepared the day before. Makes 6 servings

INDEX

(Recipes are listed according to subject)

STARTERS AND SALADS

SOUPS

VEGETABLES AND SIDE DISHES

EGGS

ONE-DISH MEALS WITH PASTA, RICE, AND GRAINS

FISH AND SHELLFISH

POULTRY

MEAT

SWEET DISHES

DRINKS